The EXECUTION of
PRIVATE SLOVIK

The EXECUTION *of* PRIVATE SLOVIK

by
William Bradford Huie

WESTHOLME
Yardley

Westholme Publishing, LLC
Eight Harvey Avenue
Yardley, Pennsylvania 19067

www.westholmepublishing.com

Printed in Canada on acid-free paper

ISBN 1-59416-003-1

First Printing
10 9 8 7 6 5 4 3 2 1

Acknowledgments . . .

A BOOK SUCH AS THIS, built paragraph by paragraph out of recollections of events long buried in military secrecy, is the work of many persons: travel, hours of conversation, hundreds of letters, endless checking and rechecking of memories.

Chief credit belongs to the nineteen men and one woman who are quoted in the text. From Antoinette Slovik to General Cota, they have submitted their actions, their opinions, to public judgment, without fear or apparent reservation. The common objective: the truth about a somber but significant event in the nation's history.

Of those not mentioned in the text, credit should go, first, to an extensive and often-criticized "bureaucracy" — the Army of the United States. Something hopeful has been happening to the army. With much of the world moving toward more secrecy, suspicion, and slavery, the army is becoming more tolerant of civilian examination. As long as pictures like *From Here to*

Eternity and books like *The Execution of Private Slovik* can be produced with the cooperation of the army, free inquirers need not lose hope. An American army, properly, has nothing to hide except weapons and battle plans.

The two army officers who deserve most credit for this book are Lieutenant Colonel James K. Gaynor, Office of the Judge Advocate General, and Captain Perry Hume Davis, II, Office of Public Information. Paul F. Gaynor, holder of the Distinguished Service Cross, now with the Central Intelligence Agency, Washington, supplied much information about the 28th Division.

A former marine, Tom Craig, of the Detroit office of the William J. Burns International Detective Agency, assisted with the research in Michigan. He reverses a pattern: many American writers are vicarious detectives; Tom Craig is a detective who can write. The manager of the Burns office in Detroit, Carl G. Munter, was also most helpful.

Mrs. Paul Stahlin, of Sanibel Island, Florida, daughter of Harry Dimmick, cooperated effectively.

To all of these, the author expresses his sincerest appreciation.

WILLIAM BRADFORD HUIE

The EXECUTION of PRIVATE SLOVIK

One . . .

On a red-and-gold autumn afternoon in 1953 I drove northeast from Paris through the "Marne country," toward those two little river valleys, the Oise and the Aisne, where already in this war-tortured, half-spent century, two waves of Americans, a generation apart, have done battle for the causes of freedom. For those of us who value the Western heritage, this is hallowed ground. Here, in 1944, youths riding with Patton rumbled over the selfsame hillocks into which their fathers had burrowed; and more than one son, spelling out the name of a village, suddenly recognized it as a bright page in his father's memories.

I drove slowly, savoring the rich, rolling countryside of the Ile-de-France: beetroot fields and birch-circled ponds; haystacks, both round and square; farmers working the powerful, brown Ardennais horses; side roads flanked with hedges, ferns and heather; old-fashioned, long-enduring homesteads. This is soil literally nourished with blood.

Fifteen miles above Château Thierry, through Belleau Wood, I spied what I had traveled to see: the Oise-Aisne American Cemetery, at Fère-en-Tardenois. The Stars and Stripes floating against a cobalt sky; lime trees and rose beds; and, through the trees, long, falling-away lines of white crosses on cultivated green. These cemeteries — there are fifteen in France alone: six First War, nine Second — are an American contribution to our times. We Americans, who span the earth in our air chariots, we plant these crosses, perhaps, as some say, in the service of an imperialism as selfish as Rome's, but perhaps, too, in the service of a genuine concern for all mankind.

I walked reverently down the avenues of crosses, past a rich variety of names and birth dates, including Sergeant Joyce Kilmer, until I stood before the massive, semicircular, colonnaded cenotaph — the central monument for these 6012 graves.

At the top of the semicircular stone wall, in foot-high letters, runs this inscription: THESE ENDURED ALL AND GAVE ALL THAT HONOR AND JUSTICE MIGHT PREVAIL AND THAT THE WORLD MIGHT ENJOY FREEDOM AND INHERIT PEACE.

At each end of the cenotaph there is a small chapel, and on one of these chapel walls, in gold letters, is this inscription: IN GRATEFUL REMEMBRANCE OF HER SONS WHO DIED IN THE WORLD WAR THIS CHAPEL IS ERECTED BY THE UNITED STATES OF AMERICA.

Between the chapels, in the center of the cenotaph, stands an altar of yellow marble; and across this altar, in both English and the more majestic French, runs still another inscription: IN SACRED SLEEP THEY REST — ILS DORMENT LEUR SOMMEIL DE GLOIRE.

But I had come to visit a particular grave, and, sadly, I realized that I would not find it in any of the four regular plots in the cemetery, Plot A, B, C or D. The grave I sought was in Plot E — a "special" plot — and to visit it I had to walk out of the cemetery proper, across the paved road, to the superintendent's cottage, and impose a formidable document, prepared in Washington, on the superintendent.

He was surprised: the existence of Plot E is a secret. There is no path leading to it. It is hidden in thick woods back of the superintendent's house, carefully surrounded with shrubs. It is a grass-covered, flat rectangle, one hundred feet long and fifty feet wide: no monuments, no inscriptions, no names. There is one small bare marble cross for four rows of graves, twenty-four graves to a row, numbered 1 to 96. The numbers, at each grave, are on 4 x 6-inch white marble blocks set into and level with the grass, the numbers engraved in black.

For the United States is ashamed of Plot E. None of the gratitude expressed on the cenotaph in the main cemetery is extended to its graves. It is the burial place of the ninety-six American soldiers executed in the

European Theater of Operations during the Second War.

Ninety-five of these ninety-six criminals were hanged by the United States for ordinary crimes of violence: murder and/or rape of unarmed civilians. I had come to visit the grave of the extraordinary criminal: the one man in the plot who was neither a murderer nor a rapist.

The card I carried said that he lay in Row 3, Grave No. 65:

PVT. EDDIE D. SLOVIK
36896415
Detroit, Michigan
Feb. 18, 1920 – Jan. 31, 1945

I stood there at his number. The dishonored grave of an American rifleman . . . a Polish Catholic boy brought up around Hamtramck. Company G. 109th Infantry. 28th Division — the old Keystone or "Bloody Bucket" — National Guard outfit from Pennsylvania.

"A good kid, Slovik . . . did anything I told him to . . . sandy-haired, blue-eyed, one-hundred-forty pounds, five-eight."

"Sure, I remember him . . . a well-setup soldier."

At that grave I had ended a long journey. I had never met Private Slovik while he was alive, but I had traveled over a continent talking with people who had known him: his mother, who knew him for seventeen of his twenty-five-years-less-eighteen-days; his wife,

[6]

who knew him for two years; a Catholic priest who knew him for two hours and who gave him the last rites; a five-star general named Eisenhower who personally signed the order resulting in his death; a famous Presbyterian preacher who saw him die; and more than two score other Americans — doctors, salesmen, a psychiatrist, lawyers, a bartender, a railroad man, two dentists, an optometrist, two major generals, farmers, a cop — all of whose lives had brushed briefly against Private Slovik's ill-starred one.

Now, there at his grave, I felt that I knew Eddie Slovik better than any of the others could have known him. . . . Better than his mother or his wife . . . better than if I had met him while he lived. It's only after a man is dead and you take the trouble to piece together his meaningful moments and reflect on them that you can know him. You can't know a man from his name and serial number; nor from his police record; nor from crouching with him in a foxhole in the dark; not even from hearing his last confession. You can't be "briefed" on a human soul. A man is not like a dog: even the simplest man is a complex, a personality . . . and you have to work to know him.

But why had I worked to know Eddie Slovik? Life is short; one has time to learn to know so few of his fellows; why had I bothered to travel so far, to ask so many questions, all just to know one dishonored Polack private from Detroit? He had been dead nearly nine years and I was the only human being on earth who had ever inquired as to the location of this grave, much less visited it. Nobody else knew Private Slovik, but why should they? Why had I bothered?

The answer is that I was one of the few reflective Americans who knew *about* Eddie Slovik: he has been a Secret. And I knew that his experience is the most unusual of any citizen who has borne arms for the United States within my lifetime.

Private Slovik is the only truly unique modern American soldier. He stands absolutely alone in his category: he is the most distinctive individual to wear the military uniform of this country in almost a century.

Private Slovik was killed *by* the United States for the crime of refusing to serve the United States with a rifle and a bayonet, for desertion to avoid the hazardous duty of close combat; and, since 1864, he is the *only* American to be executed for such an offense.

His distinction goes beyond the military: in "modern times" he is the only American, either soldier or civilian, to be put to death for a crime of omission . . . for a failure . . . for a refusal to perform an assigned duty.

Private Slovik drew the issue clearly between himself and the United States. He felt that the United States had wronged him. He claimed that the United States had made unfair demands on his private person; that he was too nervous to stay in the line; that he hated guns; that he lacked the temperament to ram a bayonet through human bodies; and, therefore, he claimed the right to place personal safety above the military purposes of the United States.

Private Slovik further claimed that more than anything on earth, including the United States, he loved his wife; that he loved their newly furnished apartment — the only warm, friendly, safe place he had ever known; that he loved to come home of a late afternoon and make love to his wife; that he loved to sit in the Carmen Theater in Dearborn, Michigan, of an evening, his lips at his wife's ear, watching a good movie; that he loved to drink a beer with her at Nick's Place; that he loved their Pontiac; that all these delights were particularly precious to him because they had been so recently acquired — he had been a depression, reform-school lad; and, therefore, since he lacked the spiritual equipment to be an effective rifleman, he insisted that the United States should allow him to serve in safety.

But the United States disagreed. Patriotic lawyers made a compelling *Case for The United States* against Private Slovik. In reviewing the action of the court and the convening authority, Major Frederick J. Bertolet, of Reading, Pennsylvania, stated:

[Private Slovik] has directly challenged the authority of the [United States], and future discipline depends upon a resolute reply to this challenge. If the death penalty is ever to be imposed for desertion it should be imposed in this case, not as a punitive measure nor as retribution, but to main-

[9]

tain that discipline upon which alone an army can succeed against the enemy.

And on a January morning in 1945, in fifteen-inch snow in the Vosges Mountains, by order of the man who is now President of the United States, Private Slovik was marched out and bound to a post. The Stars and Stripes was presented; the order expressing the will of the people of the United States was read; four chaplains representing all our faiths joined in prayer; and twelve American private soldiers raised M-1 rifles, took aim, and "shot the accused coward to death with musketry."

Thus Private Eddie D. Slovik assumes his singular position in the annals of freedom: he is the only authentic, adjudged, actually executed American coward in the Age of Freud.

2

Eddie Slovik stands alone at the losing end of an intriguing downward progression.

During the Second War, when free America mobilized its manpower against totalitarian challenge, one youth out of every eight was excused from military service "for reasons other than physical." These were not the boys with bad hearts, bad eyes, or bad feet, but the boys with bad minds: their number was 1,532,500 — the temperamentally unstable, the maladjusted, the sexually perverted, and the overly nervous.

Thus one eighth of the physically-fit products of our little-demanding society were mentally unfit to assume any responsibility whatever in the bloody business of killing the enemy.

Of the 10,110,103 who were inducted, only 2,670,000 were trained for actual ground combat; and of these a very large number, believed to be as high as a million men, soon managed to escape combat by such devices as bad-conduct discharges, or self-inflicted wounds, or by being excused by psychiatrists for some form of mental insufficiency.

Among those who evaded combat were about forty thousand who were believed to have "taken off" or "bugged out" or "deserted before the enemy." * Most of these were tried by lesser courts-martial and confined in the disciplinary training centers or dishonorably discharged. A total of 2864, however, were tried by general courts-martial, and these received sentences of from twenty years to death. And of the death sentences decreed by the general courts, forty-nine were approved by what is known in military law as the "convening authority."

* The reference here is only to those men charged with the grave offense of "desertion before the enemy" — running off during or immediately prior to combat — not to those charged with the relatively minor offenses of overstaying leave, drunkenness, AWOL from training camps.

Thus: 40,000 deserters — 49 approved death sentences.

But such death sentences — since the Civil War — have not actually been executed. Not in the Indian wars; not in the Spanish American War; not in the First War; not in the Second War; not in the Korean War. Despite all the heavy sentences, nobody was shot to death — and, at least during the Second and Korean wars, there were few who believed that anybody would be shot to death. And this was because it was widely held that the people of the United States no longer demanded — indeed, would no longer tolerate — the extreme penalty for a citizen who refused to fight. So the military representatives of the United States followed a practice of commuting the death sentences, reducing the prison sentences systematically, and releasing the deserters shortly after the wars were over.

This was the practice in every case *except one*. No deserter was actually shot *except Private Slovik*.

On Armistice Day, 1944, with the 28th Division bloodily engaged in Hürtgen Forest, a division court-martial gave Slovik the death sentence. On November 27, 1944, the division commander, one of the great field soldiers of the war, Major General Norman D. "Dutch" Cota, approved the sentence. Nothing unusual or surprising to this point.

The unusual began in Paris. There, with increasing numbers of American deserters in his prisons near or inside the city, General Eisenhower took solemn counsel; and on December 23, 1944, he decided to give final confirmation to a death sentence for desertion. The last American to assume final responsibility in such a case had been Abraham Lincoln; the last West Pointer, acting for the United States, had been General Winfield Scott.

The name on the execution order: Private Eddie D. Slovik.

3

But why was it Slovik? What was there about this dead-end kid to win him such a role in a nation's history? Are there giant wheels that start turning somewhere, long before a man is born, which eventually deliver him, alone among millions, before a dozen aimed rifles in fifteen-inch snow?

Of all those three-million-odd Mental Insufficients, of all those thousands of deserters, of all those deserters who were sentenced to death, of the forty-nine whose death sentences were approved, was Slovik the very worst offender? The only one to whom the United States could not extend clemency?

And what of the United States? Of all those who had challenged its authority, was Slovik's challenge the *one* which demanded the most resolute reply? Had the United States, at crisis, been so humiliated and handicapped by its cowards that it had to reach out and smash one of them with its great hand in an effort to make the others accept their responsibilities?

I began asking myself such questions in 1946 when I first learned of what came to be marked in my files as the Fascinating Statistic: thousands guilty — *one man* shot. I didn't then discover the name of the man who had been shot, or any of the circumstances, but I typed this note and stuck it into the file:

The *one man* in such a situation always deserves to be known. Some day I must dig him up. I must also examine the significance of the fact that in its struggle to inspirit its youth, to discipline them, to make them stand and fight, the United States resorted, as late as 1945, to *one* full-dress execution.

Throughout the Second War I had been interested in this struggle between a nation which seemed unsure of itself and its reluctant soldiery. This war was particularly cruel to the individual: it was never presented as a crusade — no music, no poems, no flags — and it's cruel to ask a man to risk his life in any war which isn't fought for the highest purpose. I understood the belly-tightening cynicism of a situation in which a few citizens are required to risk everything while practically everybody else gets promoted, "enjoys the war," and makes himself richer and more comfortable. I knew that impulse up there in the dark to fail to hear the command to advance; to stay in the hole, head down, while

[14]

others pressed on; to try to assure the safe return to love, warm beds, tile baths, life, and privacy.

I also knew some of the difficulties of the United States. I remembered a night in the summer of 1940 when I sat in a tent in Louisiana with a pensive George S. Patton, Jr.

"Yes, by god, I *am* worried," the general said. "I'm worried because I'm not sure this country can field a fighting army at this stage in our history. We've pampered and confused our youth. We've talked too much about rights and not enough about duties. Now we've got to try to make them attack and kill. A big percentage of our men won't be worth a goddam to us. Many a brave soldier will lose his life unnecessarily because the man next to him turns yellow. We're going to have to dig down deep to find our hard core of scrappers. That takes time; and time is short. I've lived my life in the shadow of the flag, and I say, God help the United States!"

Well, fate again provided time enough. We excused or discharged or hospitalized or imprisoned our Insufficients; brave men died needlessly when their buddies stayed in the holes and failed to sustain them; we dug down and found our hard core of scrappers; they fought magnificently; and we so chronicled their exploits that the "other story" — the story of the struggle between the United States and the reluctant youths — was obscured. The people at home heard a few ugly

[15   ]

noises from behind the woodshed: "the psychiatrists are decimating our army in North Africa"; "Patton slapped a sick man"; "a colonel named Jim Kilian has allowed brutes from Harlan County, Kentucky, to beat up Americans in the Lichfield guardhouse" — but I thought their significance was not understood.

So after the war, when I learned that there had been one execution, I began a sort of once-a-year effort to persuade various persons in authority at the Pentagon to de-classify the case and to co-operate with me in its presentation.

The long argument, renewed almost annually and conducted by several sincere spokesmen for the defense establishment, contained such points as these:

THE PENTAGON: Huie, what-the-hell good can come of digging that thing up? . . . Don't we have enough trouble? . . . Some professor is always writing a piece for a magazine implying that everybody concerned with justice in the army is either a sadist or a martinet. . . . Now you want to scare every mama in the country by dramatizing how we shot one poor guy who fouled up. . . . How can that story possibly do the army any good? . . . And what about the family of this man who was shot? Shouldn't we protect them from embarrassment? . . .

HUIE: Sir, you may be correct, but I urge you to consider these points. . . . The fact that you have executed only one man for a military offense in ninety years is hardly an indication of sadism. . . . The story, told honestly, will bring only sympathy for this man's family. . . . The United States didn't shoot him as a punishment: that isn't the first purpose of military justice. His execution was staged as a hoped-for deterrent. But doesn't secrecy limit deterrent value? . . . The interest of the United States is transcendent here. I think the United States may be confused over what it can properly demand of a citizen. I remember what my great-grandmother said in 1934 to one of my cousins who was trying to collect his First War bonus. "Son," she said, "the United States of America don't owe you a damn cent for fighting in its wars." That position is out of date, but why is this nation so reluctant to expect patriotism and loyalty and sacrifice as its due? It seems afraid to ask its citizens to fight for it or even work for it in safety, except at inflated wages with triple time for overtime. . . . There were men who deserted during the Second War and during the Korean War because they were confused as to what the United States has a right to demand of them. . . . If this story is what I think it may be, then it can be a useful dramatic device for causing people to think and decide. It can help toward a new understanding between the United States and the individual citizen.

One afternoon in July, 1953, I sat in the Office of the

Judge Advocate General in the Pentagon with two officers — a lieutenant colonel and a major general. I again stated my request, but this time there was no argument. When I had finished, the general gazed out over the Potomac for a moment, then turned and spoke softly.

"Colonel, clear this with the Office of Public Information and see that every document we have in this case is made available to Mr. Huie and his publishers."

In twenty minutes I had what I had been seeking for seven years. A property of red tape, often forgotten, is that it dissolves miraculously before secure, intelligent authority.

A week later, in a remote little restaurant near Wayne, Michigan, where we were the only customers, I met a nervous but remarkable woman, Antoinette Slovik. She had been frightened by the strange voice over the telephone which wanted to discuss her late husband in confidence, but she had come alone to the rendezvous.

"I'm interested, as a writer, in the story of Eddie Slovik," I said. "I have documents and information that I will give you. But first will you tell me what you know about his death?"

"I've lived for eight years with little information," she replied. "A telegram said that my husband had 'died in the European Theater of Operations.' I sent copies of it to Eddie's mother, his sisters, his parole officers. A little later, when I wrote to inquire about the insurance, I got a note saying the insurance would not be paid because my husband had died 'under dishonorable circumstances.' Until now I've never mentioned that note to a living soul. I've kept it inside myself and it's been like a cancer, making me sick."

I told her as much as I knew then; I explained what I wanted to do; I asked for her help.

"Yes, I'll help," she said. "If this had to happen to one man among thousands in ninety years, I could have told you that Eddie Slovik would be the one. He was the unluckiest poor kid who ever lived. I don't know what publication of this story will do to me. Maybe I'll have to leave here. But I'll help. You can have his letters, his pictures, every memory of mine. If the people of the United States killed him, I'd like for a few of them to know the man they killed and how much trouble we had."

4

Now, as I stood there at the grave, in the dishonored plot reserved for criminals, the story was finished. The manuscript, checked and rechecked by the army, by Antoinette Slovik, by almost everyone mentioned in it, had been delivered to the publishers.

"Well, Eddie," I mused, "I guess that's about it. You remember that little priest, Father Cummings, who prayed for you while you stood there waiting for the volley? He told me that you are now a Conscious Being out there Somewhere. If you are, then you know that I've dug you up. I've done my best to re-create you as you were. . . . One of the chaps in your firing squad said to me: 'You know I've often wondered about that guy we shot — what'd you say his name was? I never saw him except that morning when he stood there in the snow with that GI blanket around his shoulders and we killed him. I wondered what that little bastard was like? How he came to foul up and catch that rap?' . . . And General Cota said to me in his office in Philadelphia: 'That execution was the roughest fifteen minutes of my life. I stood there and faced the man, witnessed his death; it was my duty. But of course I never knew him, except what the record showed.'

"Now, Eddie, they can all know you — everybody from the privates in the firing squad up to the President. . . . If you are that Conscious Being, you can know them. . . . And quite a few thoughtful Americans, in whose name you were shot to death, can now sit in judgment on Private Slovik — and on the United States."

Two . . .

As Private Slovik stood with his execution party, waiting to march out into the courtyard, an MP sergeant, Frank J. McKendrick, of Philadelphia, said to him: "Try to take it easy, Eddie. Try to make it easy on yourself — and on us."

"Don't worry about me," Slovik replied. "I'm okay. They're not shooting me for deserting the United States Army — thousands of guys have done that. They're shooting me for bread I stole when I was twelve years old."

And after Slovik had been pronounced dead by Dr. Robert E. Rougelot, of New Orleans, the Graves Registration detail which claimed his body found in his pocket a small address book containing eight addresses, printed in pencil. One of these was:

> H. Dimmick,
> 330 E. Main St.,
> Ionia, Michigan.

So you have to drive to Ionia to begin knowing Eddie Slovik. On the map it's a town of six or seven thousand in the fertile farm country a hundred miles west of Detroit. But "Ionia," when spoken, is usually not in reference to a town but to the Michigan Reformatory located there.

The institution sits on a hilltop, like an old, mottled, medieval castle. You can see it for miles as you approach. It overlooks hundreds of acres of farmlands worked by its inmates. Its immediate grounds — green lawns and thousands of blooming flowers — are overshadowed by the dark walls. In the center is a circular control room, from which the cell blocks extend like spokes in a wheel. Around the cell blocks, the rim of the wheel, runs the outside wall, with its catwalks and guard towers. The normal population is 1300: ages 15 to 23.

You learn that Harry Dimmick, after twenty-five years as a supervisor at the reformatory, has been off duty for several months, following a heart attack. So you go to his cottage: he now lives at 734 E. Main. He is a heavy, pleasant, balding man with white hair, near sixty, his breath still short from the thrombosis. He smiles readily, compassionately: not the motion-picture prison guard. You converse for a moment; then, in a generous gesture to save a traveler's time, Harry Dimmick tells you he's going to try to round up one or two other supervisors who remember Eddie Slovik . . . and soon you're one of a little group in the cottage . . . and the several of you sit there talking, smoking, remembering, evaluating.

These "supervisors" are realists. They don't deal with well-scrubbed, well-adjusted, soundly motivated boys from secure homes. They spend their lives working to straighten misbent twigs; and, like baseball players trying to bat .300, they toil with the limited objective of "25 per cent remissions" — struggling to make a good citizen of one lad out of four.

First, these men, and especially Harry Dimmick, are saddened to learn that a noxious distinction has come to Ionia: it's now the *one* twig-straightening institution in the country with the *one* alumnus to be shot for desertion.

—— This is all very surprising to us, they agree. We had no idea that Eddie died in this fashion. His wife wrote us that he had been killed, and we stuck a gold star next to his name on our armed-service board. That was sort of misrepresenting things, wasn't it? But we didn't know any better. Since we had him here for almost five years, guess this doesn't speak too well for us.

—— It's a big surprise, too, that it was Eddie. We thought he had a pretty good chance to make it. He sent us invitations to his wedding: he was so proud of his wife. We thought he'd make it because he wasn't a cop-hater. He was a friendly, goodhearted kid. Sort of

a lone wolf . . . never laughed much, or played jokes
. . . but he never had a fight while he was here . . .
never made an enemy. Weak as dishwater, sure, scared,
insecure . . . but we thought he had a good chance because he didn't hate.

—— Now if it had been his brother, Raymond, we
wouldn't be so surprised. We had them both here. Ray
after Eddie . . . even though Ray is two years older.
Ray came up on an arson rap, five to twenty years. Ray's
like iron: a wiry, hot-headed little Polack cop-hater.
Give him a bottle of beer, bat your eye and he could
beat your brains out. If the army had taken Ray, he
might have won the Congressional Medal, or he might
have shot up six MPs and his commanding officer. But
that's Ray Slovik, not Eddie. Eddie was weak and soft,
scared but gentle. It's hard to figure Eddie before a
firing squad . . . damned hard.

—— Or maybe it *does* figure . . . if you look at it
from another angle. This is different from the civilian
executions we deal with; it's different from the usual
army execution. The normal execution is for violence;
but Eddie's was for running away from a fight.

—— Sure . . . when you consider it like that . . . it
figures. We could have predicted that Eddie might run.
When we said that we thought he had a good chance
to make it, we were talking about civilian life. We
didn't mean that he was a good bet to hold a firing line
in the dark.

The record? Edward Donald Slovik arrived at Ionia December 27, 1937, transferred from the state prison at Jackson because of his age: two months shy of eighteen. He had been sentenced October 1, 1937, to a term of six months to ten years for embezzlement. He had confessed to pocketing change received over the counter of Cunningham Drug Store, Woodward and Owens Streets, Detroit, in which he was working — also to taking home candy, chewing gum, and cigarets without paying. The total amount named in the complaint was $59.60, accumulated over a six-month period.

During his first 14 days at Ionia Eddie was kept in quarantine, or solitary, as are all new prisoners, pending results of physical and psychiatric examinations. The recorded findings: 66 inches tall; 138 pounds; clear, blue eyes; sandy hair; good general health; pronounced acne about the face and neck; bad tonsils; 22–30 vision, left eye; needed dental work; negative Wassermann; alert; mentally clear; exhibited no unusual behavior; although he did not lie, in answering certain questions he appeared to be withholding comment, particularly about his home life; well-integrated thought processes; no psychosis; prognosis, favorable.

Born of Polish parents on Edwin Street; substandard neighborhood; father, Josef Slowikowski, born in Poland, mother in U.S., second marriage for father;

father a punch-press operator intermittently employed at Briggs — auto bodies; one brother, three sisters; completed eighth grade, part of ninth; attended Dickerson and Kosciusko schools, Hamtramck; Davidson and Pulaski schools, Detroit; could read, write and spell satisfactorily; quit school when he turned fifteen.

Conduct invariably that of his associates: when they drank he drank; when they stayed out all night he stayed out all night; when they stole he stole. Probably began petty thefts when he was ten or eleven, by filching bread and cake from his first employer, a baker. First entry on police blotter 1932, when he was twelve: he and his pals broke into the basement of a brass foundry. They were going to steal some brass but decided to build a bonfire first. Smoke attracted the beat cop. Eddie was put on one year's probation for breaking and entering. From '32 to '37, when he was first sent up, recurrent offenses included petty theft, more B & E, disturbing the peace, always with associates.

At Ionia Eddie Slovik was first put to work in the prison electrical shop, but he didn't satisfy his supervisor. He was transferred to the auto shop. In March, 1938, he was eligible for parole, but the board recommended that in view of his juvenile record he be detained to establish a good work record at Ionia.

On July 20, 1938, he again came before the parole board, and it was decided that his home environment was such that he should not be returned to it. However,

[26]

he was paroled on September 9, 1938, with a good-conduct record and two years probational-parole time to serve.

Prison records reveal that no one visited Eddie Slovik on any occasion during his first stretch at Ionia.

Upon leaving prison he went to work in a chain grocery store, reported regularly to his parole officer, and was not arrested for four months. Then one night he and two pals beered up and stole a car "just to go for a ride." They skidded on an ice patch and smashed the car against a brick building. Eddie ran away from the wreck, but turned himself in to the police later that same night.

Next day, January 20, 1939, in recorder's court, he pleaded guilty to unlawfully driving away an automobile and violation of parole; sentenced to two and a half to seven and a half years; sent to Jackson Prison; transferred in March to Ionia.

This time Eddie was assigned to work in the furniture factory. In the second month he was reported by his supervisor for stealing a bottle of denatured alcohol, after which he was transferred to another supervisor in another section of the furniture factory.

That, in Eddie Slovik's judgment, was his first good fortune. He had stolen the alcohol, he said, not to drink but to rub on his legs at night. At birth his legs had been grotesquely bowed, and there had been an operation, with the bones broken in several places, to straighten them. This left scars and recurring pain and always caused him to wear the lightest shoes he could get. In the only photograph of him with his training company at Camp Wolters, Texas, he is sitting next to his commanding officer, conspicuous as the only man in the company wearing, by special permission, light slippers, not the regulation GI shoes.

But what made the alcohol theft a blessing for Eddie was that the new supervisor to whom he was transferred was — Harry Dimmick. That's how they met. And Dimmick was the professional twig-straightener whom Eddie credited with straightening him out. From the moment he met Harry Dimmick until he fouled up in the army, Eddie had no further trouble with the law; and he carried Dimmick's name in his pocket to his reckoning day, when the United States settled accounts with him in the Vosges Mountains.

3

—— I had Eddie for almost three years, Harry Dimmick recalls — from about May, 1939, until April, 1942, when he was paroled to go to work for that plumbing company in Detroit. I never had a boy I liked more. He was goodhearted, a good worker, and, with a little luck, I figured he could make a pretty good citizen.

—— I trained him to be a wood finisher, and him and me and a couple of the other boys used to travel in the car to the various state-owned institutions, to repair

[28   ]

and paint the furniture. We'd be gone four or five days at a time. I talked to Eddie a lot. I trusted him. And he never violated a trust, never gave me a minute's trouble.

—— I remember a thing that happened one night that may show you what he lacked. I had Eddie and two of the other boys with me and we were working at the state hospital for the insane — repairing and painting furniture. The four of us were sleeping on cots on the top floor — the other two boys in the room with me, and Eddie just outside the door on the screened-in porch. Just as we were going to bed, a patient broke loose somewhere and ran screaming down the corridor. It made all the boys a little jittery, but Eddie much more than the other two. Then we all went to sleep. But two or three hours later one of the boys waked up and decided to play a joke on Eddie. We have a lot of that, you know: boys always playing jokes on each other: some of them pretty rough.

—— Well, this boy sneaks off his cot and out to where Eddie is asleep. He crawls right up to Eddie's ear and lets out a hellacious scream. Eddie, of course, jumps up like he's been shot, and the other boys get a big laugh.

—— It scared hell out of Eddie. He got out of bed, shaking like a leaf, and made the boy who had played the joke on him exchange places with him. Eddie brought his cot right in next to mine. He was still shaking after we turned the light off, so I reached over and held him by the hand a minute or so until he went back to sleep.

—— That's all we try to do for these fouled-up kids — just reach out a hand and try to give them a little strength that they don't have.

—— I'm not going to offer any excuses for Eddie Slovik. A man's a man, and he stands up to life as best he can and takes what's dished out to him. Men in my business don't offer excuses for boys; we just try to help. But if you want to understand Eddie Slovik as he *was* — and not as he ought to have been — then you've got to understand a few things about the United States.

—— Men in my business know that there are good years and bad years to be born in this country. It's like those good years and bad years for wine in France. There are good years and bad years to be born in a city like Detroit. And, brother, let's face it: if your old man was a Polack punch-press operator for Briggs, 1920 was a *bad* year to be born. Here at Ionia we know all about the Class of 1920 — and '21, and '22, and '23. Those might have been prosperous years for the United States, but they were bad years for babies.

—— If you were born in 1920 and your old man was a punch-press operator, then when you were ten and eleven and twelve and thirteen and fourteen, your old man didn't punch much bcause Briggs couldn't sell many fenders to Ford or General Motors or Chrysler . . . because they couldn't sell many cars. Your old man had plenty of time to lie at home drunk and beat up the kids and the old woman; your mother couldn't get much scrubbing to do for other folks, so she had time to drink and fight while the kids foraged in the street. The welfare paid your rent; Briggs provided a little scrip to buy potatoes with; and, if you were twelve years old in that situation in 1932, then everybody you knew was hungry and fighting and stealing and drinking and in trouble. And you were scared. And you came out of it — unless you were unusual — either weak and scared and feeling inferior, or else rebellious and resentful and full of hate, wanting to fight and maybe kill somebody.

—— Eddie Slovik came out of it weak and scared and feeling inferior . . . a petty thief . . . a "con" who knew he'd always be, at best, an "ex-con."

—— What can you do with a boy like that? You talk to him, try to build him up. You straighten him out with the law. That's what I did. On August 6, 1940, I sent a favorable report to the parole board. I said that he was trustworthy and a good worker. The board recommended that he be discharged from his sentence for violation of parole, and this was done on September 16, 1940. Then he began doing time for the automobile theft.

—— The next thing you do for a boy like that is try to teach him to use his hands so he can make a living. You help him get some sort of job. . . . Then you turn him loose . . . and keep your fingers crossed. You make him report to his parole officer every month so you can watch him as best you can . . . and you hope he meets folks outside — particularly a woman — who can hold him by the hand and supply some of what he needs.

—— That's what we did, as best we could, for Eddie Slovik. When he walked out of here in April, 1942, he was twenty-two years old; in good health; a nice-looking, clean-cut one-hundred-forty-pounder, with a friendly smile, showing good teeth. He wasn't mad at nobody — except a little resentment toward his folks; all he had hanging over him was two years probational time; he had a job waiting for him at fifty cents an hour; and all he had to do was get himself a new environment, stay away from bad company, find himself a good woman, work hard, go to church, report to his parole officer once a month, and not get drunk. It sounds like a large order — and just one out of four makes it — but I thought Eddie had a good chance.

—— The army? It wasn't a problem for him — except that it added to his feeling of inferiority. He was automatically 4–F, like all our boys. The United States knew he wasn't good soldier material. But, in some ways, this gave him advantages: good jobs were plentiful; there wasn't so much competition for the good women. He could go out and work hard, find a strong woman, get promoted, and save his money during the war boom. By the end of the war he could have himself established.

—— And I'm not going to criticize the United States

for shooting him. What happened over there across the water I don't know enough about. I voted for General Eisenhower for President; I think he's a great American. If Eisenhower sent Eddie Slovik before a firing squad, he must have had a sound reason for doing it. When you've got a big war to win, you don't have time to give too much consideration to one weak little man.

—— But I could have told the general this. I could have said, General, you can take Eddie Slovik and put a suit on him and teach him how to march in step. You can hand him a gun and try to teach him how to shoot it. You can march him up to the battle line and make him dig a hole. But I can tell you *exactly* what he's going to do. When it gets dark and the first shell bursts over his head, if *somebody stronger than he is is not there to hold him by the hand,* he's sure going to do one of two things. He's either going to freeze right there in the bottom of that hole, or else he's going to jump out and run like a scared rabbit. And there's nothing you can tell him — and not much you can do — to prevent it.

—— We had time to help him a little at Ionia — but we didn't get him until he was eighteen years old! We only had time to teach him to quit stealing, to look neat, to work at a job. We didn't have time to instill big things like patriotism down in his guts.

—— When he left us he was a fair risk not to cause the United States any more trouble in fair weather.

[33]

But he was a poor risk to stand fast in the dark with guns roaring around him.

—— We knew this . . . and the army knew it: that's why they had him in 4–F.

4

In April, 1942, then twenty-two-year-old Eddie Slovik walked through the main gate at Ionia, wearing a new suit, carrying in a bundle under his arm all his possessions, and, in his pocket, a five-dollar bill.

It was a different United States than he had faced when he was twelve or seventeen. It was a different Detroit. Depression had retreated before wartime prosperity. Detroit was no longer a Disaster Area; it was now the bustling Arsenal of Democracy. Punch-press operators were punching overtime . . . at triple time. Everywhere there was opportunity for a youth who would work and who didn't have to go to the army: the opportunities of war . . . the opportunities to acquire precious things like privacy — a private apartment, a private automobile, a private woman.

There were delicious opportunities for a weak, scared, depression kid who had done time for petty thievery: opportunities to build himself up . . . to get what was coming to him — everything anybody else had . . . and, by the end of the war, to have something, to be secure.

The United States was prosperous . . . and the only fly in the prosperity was that a few men had to go off to unpleasant places and die. So professors had been summoned to Washington and put to work, overtime, devising orientation courses, explaining to American youth Why-We-Fight . . . why Arnold von Winkelried gathered the spears into his particular, private breast . . . why those particular Three Hundred stood in the pass at Thermopylae . . . why that ragged, hungry few endured at Valley Forge.

The United States was prosperous . . . and also in peril. Patriotism had become corny; the ancient virtues had become suspect; and under massive assault throughout the world was the original idea of the United States: the idea that one man is important, and godlike, and worthy to be free, and capable of big things like sacrifice and devotion, love and responsibility.

While Eddie Slovik had been in prison, being taught not to steal, great battles had been fought. The Battle of Britain — a few men in airplanes with hearts and hands set against the enemy; Bataan and Corregidor. The marines were approaching Guadalcanal! Torpedo Eight was preparing to die to the last man at Midway; the desert rats were retreating to victory at El Alamein.

But these were things too big for the curriculum at Ionia. And neither Ionia nor heredity nor previous environment had equipped Eddie Slovik to be a responsible custodian, a proud inheritor, or a resolute defender of the faith. Harry Dimmick's hope for him had been wisely measured: that he could find a woman on the outside who would clutch him by the hand and supply some of the strength that he didn't have.

Three . . .

EDDIE SLOVIK found his woman in a plumbing shop: the Montella Plumbing Company, 5522 Shaeffer Road, Dearborn, Michigan: James Montella, proprietor. Mr. Montella had several small children, who were cared for by a housekeeper, Margaret Slovik, Eddie's older sister. And Mr. Montella's bookkeeper was an ambitious, twenty-seven-year-old Polish girl with a strong will and a weak body: Antoinette Wisniewski.

Margaret Slovik, of course, knew Antoinette Wisniewski, and early in 1942 they discussed a problem. Miss Slovik had a brother at Ionia who was coming up for parole. He needed some responsible person to write a letter to the parole board offering a job. The two women persuaded Mr. Montella to offer the job — fifty cents an hour as a plumber's helper — and Antoinette Wisniewski wrote the letter.

Thus Antoinette Wisniewski reached out a hand to Eddie Slovik even before she had met him: she began by helping him get out of jail.

Eddie reported to work the morning after he had left Ionia. His sister brought him in, smiling but uneasy in his new gray suit, and introduced him to Mr. Montella and to Antoinette Wisniewski.

Two years later, from Camp Wolters, Eddie wrote:

The first day I saw you there at Montella's plumbing shop I knew you was the dream girl I had been dreaming of while I was in jail. You remember how I use to stand there watching you? I knew I loved you and needed you. You know I always watched you wherever you went and whenever you was walking. I admired you. I said I fell in love with your purty legs and your figure. Well, darling, that's the truth. When I first talked to you I was sure I wanted you. I fought to make you love me. You even lied to me to get rid of me but I hung around. I couldn't let you go. I couldn't wait till my day's work was done to hurry up to the shop and take you to Nick's for dinner. And then to the Carmen for a show.

Even though he worked in overalls and dug ditches for sewers, the plumbing shop was the center of a delightful new world for the graduate of Edwin Street and Ionia. He quickly learned that Dearborn was not the Detroit he had known, that the Wisniewskis were not the Sloviks; and he yearned to move to Dearborn and the Wisniewskis.

Dearborn is a city of small-home owners. It is free of the vast, brawling slum areas of Detroit and Hamtramck, where the marginal workers beer up and beat each other's brains out, where the welfare pays the rent, where everybody is in trouble, and where there are more cheap bars per linear foot than in any other city in the world. Dearborn is the mecca of the Polish artisan who works steady, owns his home, goes to church, eats ham hocks and sauerkraut, and smiles at the thought of his son playing tackle for Notre Dame.

His first visit to the Wisniewski home at 5938 Kendal Street impressed Eddie: it was his first entrance into a house owned by the tenant — and this old brew is still potent to Sloviks. He wanted Father Wisniewski to become his father; he wanted Mother Wisniewski to become his mother: they were comfortable, friendly folks, unafraid. And most of all he wanted Antoinette. She was a woman a man could get somewhere with: she had a head on her shoulders; she could earn as much money as a man; she was five years older than he was; she could *manage;* she could be the strong hand he needed, both wife and mother; she could help satisfy all the voracious yearnings and appetites of a physically healthy, affection-starved youngster who had spent the years from eighteen to twenty-two behind bars.

But Antoinette was not to be had easily. She was a far more complex personality than was Eddie Slovik. Some of the cards had been stacked against her, too. She was not unattractive: dark-haired, brown-eyed, deep-bosomed, a full, sensual mouth; but she had been born with one leg three inches shorter than the other.

[38   ]

Then infantile paralysis had further impaired her ability to walk, and she lived with the ghost of epileptic seizure.

All these had only intensified her passion for love and possession, for privacy and independence. She had left high school to learn how to make money in offices. Her yearnings were so deep and fierce they almost choked her: a home of her own, children, luxurious furniture, nice clothes, perfumes, unguents, a powerful automobile, and a man she could possess . . . a man who could love, bring her red roses, devote himself industriously to her requirements . . . a man whom she could *manage* to Success.

Antoinette had other prospects: in fact, she was engaged to another man when she met Eddie Slovik. And while she liked Eddie from the start, she had no intention of marrying him until she made certain that he was not a hopeless weakling, that he was a good bet to produce, to satisfy her, to help her get what she wanted. She first encouraged him to leave the home of his parents — the environment from which he had gone to Ionia — and he rented a room in Dearborn near her. She watched him with liquor, and was pleased to note that he had little desire and no stomach for whisky: he was a one- or two-beer man. She watched him work, and here the promise was excellent. In addition to his ditch-digging he dressed the windows at Montella's, cleaned the floors, made himself so handy that he got raises every two or three weeks, very quickly went from

50 cents an hour to $1.05, with time-and-a-half for over-time . . . except that the overtime interfered with his courting.

She tried his devotion by fire. She craftily deceived him, kept him dangling, miserable, while she met and appraised her other suitor. Once he threatened to violate his parole, run off to Chicago, unless she gave him an answer. She cajoled him, went off herself on a vacation to make up her mind. His letters from camp recall the anguished uncertainty of his campaign to win her.

She accompanied him to his draft board, where his classification in 4–F was confirmed, with no apparent likelihood that it would be changed. She began a correspondence with Harry Dimmick, received his professional judgment that Eddie was a good bet, that army service was unlikely. In September, 1942, she went with him to his parole officer, and they asked for permission to be married.

The parole officer questioned them at length, tried to discourage them. He pointed out the differences in age, in education, in earnings, in previous modes of life. But when Eddie refused to be discouraged, the officer agreed to investigate Antoinette and to notify them by mail of the decision. A week later the letter came through: official approval.

Then came their first visit to the Sloviks on Russell Street. It was the last Sunday in September. The purpose of the visit was not only for Antoinette to meet Eddie's father and mother, but also for her to extend the invitation, traditional with Polish people, for the groom's parents to dine with the bride's parents, after which there would be a joint announcement of betrothal. Eddie's father was asleep: he worked the night shift at Briggs, and there were signs of an arduous Saturday night. He got up, talked briefly, took the invitation under advisement, went back to sleep. The mother, Anna Slovik, a muscular, harassed woman, was cool, offered no comment on the proposed marriage.

There was, of course, never a chance for anything more than limited civility between Antoinette Wisniewski and Anna Slovik. To Antoinette the Slovik parents represented all the weakness she despised and feared, the enemy she had to keep Eddie away from. And to Anna Slovik this "crippled witch" was much too old for Eddie, much too crippled, an evil influence who would devour a boy, turn him against his folks, make him wait on her hand and foot, and force him to spend his last penny on red roses for her pleasure.

The visit was less than successful, but wedding plans were made, Eddie begged his parents, and on the last Sunday in October the Slowikowskis of Detroit came to dine with the Wisniewskis of Dearborn. Uneasiness dissolved in the authoritative potables; friendliness arrived with the succulent roast. Mr. Slovik told about the punch press at Briggs; Mr. Wisniewski matched him with the open-hearth furnace at Great Lakes Steel.

The wedding date was set for November 7, 1942.

2

For a Polish wedding celebration, a man, it seems, needs his strength. These Slowikowski-Wisniewski nuptials featured seventy-two consecutive hours of unrestrained gluttony, an overworked basement bar, two hundred guests, a hired nickelodeon, and the furniture moved out to provide maneuver room for "The Beer Barrel Polka."

Because she had been the puny one, Antoinette was her mother's favorite among the four daughters, so the mother had dug into the savings to make this wedding memorable. And Antoinette had wanted a grand affair, not only for herself — a girl marries the first time only once — but also for Eddie. She wanted her little man to forget his prison denims and his sewer denims, to feel white silk and a bat-wing collar at his throat, to stand in solemn ceremony in a decorated church, to begin to think of himself as a citizen and family man with friends and responsibilities.

Eddie needed this boost, because during the planning of the wedding he had taken another right cross to the ego. His parents were Roman Catholic, and it was assumed that all the children were Catholic, too. Eddie's youngest sister was in a convent on Staten Island, New

York. Eddie had never been devout, but he had taken Communion, gone to confession, and never doubted that, while not a good one, he was, indeed, a Roman Catholic. The Wisniewskis were Roman Catholic in good standing at St. Barbara's Church, Dearborn.

However, when he and Antoinette went to St. Barbara's to arrange for their wedding, it was discovered that he could not qualify as a Roman Catholic. When he was a baby his parents had spent a while in Minnesota, and there he had been baptized in some church other than Roman Catholic. Therefore, they could not be married in St. Barbara's, nor in any other Roman Catholic church.

Eddie received this news from the priest with such bitterness . . . he was so appalled by his own sense of inadequacy . . . that he threatened to run away. In one of his letters from camp he wrote:

I was just thinking tonight of the time we went to St. Barbara's and they wouldn't let me get married there and I was ready to leave town. You begged me to stop at Scenic's for a beer and we had a beer and after talking to you I knew you loved me. You fought to hold me, didn't you?

Antoinette recalls the incident in this manner:
—— We wanted so much to get married at St. Barbara's. As Eddie had been given to understand by his parents that he was a Roman Catholic, he had lived the

[43   ]

life of one. When the investigation by the priest revealed that he wasn't a Roman Catholic, it just about killed him. Knowing that I was born and raised a Roman Catholic, he had come to the conclusion that he couldn't and wouldn't ask me to give up my religion to marry him.

—— It was a cold October night when we were returning from the church. We were walking. We didn't either of us have a car at that time. And he was so terribly depressed. I asked him if he wouldn't stop at the Scenic Inn on Ford Road. The place is still operating. We sat over in the corner and had a beer and he was cursing his parents for having lied to him. He threatened to get even with them.

—— I was afraid he might do something foolish and be returned to prison as a parole violator. He had told me that he never wanted to get back behind those walls, but that night he said: "Maybe I ought to go back to jail and forget about it all. I have no home, no parents to speak of, no religion, and the one thing I want most in life I can't have. I'll take you home tonight and when we part it will be for the last time."

—— I began to talk to him, and I told him that he meant so much to me that I'd give up my religion to marry him. The music box helped, too. It began playing "Tangerine" and "Give Me One Dozen Roses," both of them tunes he loved. His mood began to change, his face lighted up, he said that he couldn't go on without me, and after that one beer he walked me home, and we parted with plans for the next day.

The wedding was arranged and performed at a small, workingman's National Catholic church, Our Saviour of Golgotha, in Detroit, where services are conducted in both Polish and English.*

The wedding day, November 7, 1942, was a Saturday, and activities began at 5:30 A.M. Antoinette had paid a French dressmaker seven hundred dollars for the gown and veil. The four bridesmaids gathered at her home to dress: two of her sisters, a niece, and Eddie's sister Margaret. Eddie's oldest sister, Annabelle, helped with the preparations.

The ceremony was at 10 A.M., with nearly two hundred guests in the decorated church. Harry Dimmick and his wife, several other supervisors at Ionia, and the parole officer had been invited. They all sent good wishes, but they were unable to attend. At eleven the party returned to the Wisniewski home, where cooks and waitresses had been hired, where the buffet was ready, the furniture had been moved, and the nickelodeon was playing.

* In similar cases the Catholic Church would, after investigation, either accept such baptism as valid or, in case of doubt, administer conditional baptism, presuming the petitioner wished to continue profession of the Catholic faith. Later, at his death, Eddie Slovik, without question, received from the Roman Catholic chaplain all the comforts of the Roman Catholic Church. Just why then was he denied the privilege of marriage at St. Barbara's? Diligent efforts on the part of Church officials in 1953 were unable to produce a complete explanation since the particular priest who handled the matter could not be identified.

"Normally at these affairs," Antoinette recalls, "the Polish mother kills herself cooking and serving. But we had decided to hire help so that all of us could be free for the dancing and mingling with the guests."

The celebration ended the following Wednesday, and the photographers, both color and conventional, recorded every highlight. The pictures show two crippled people, more elegantly dressed than they had ever been before or would ever be again, smiling and posturing among simple, dowdy folk, trying to feel that they would bring to this marriage love, honor, and "everything that everybody else has."

In these wedding pictures Eddie Slovik looks thin and blond. Where the camera catches him from the side he looks thin-chested. He has a high forehead; his light, sandy hair is straight, parted slightly to the right of the midline, combed straight back. His chin is square and dimpled, his lips thin, particularly when drawn over his prominent teeth in a smile. His hands and forearms seem large for his size. The impression is of a little man who must work at smiling to keep from crying — who must always be at Nick's having a beer, or at the Carmen, or nervously at work, or humming "Tangerine," or clutching at someone, or having himself built up, lest he fall prey to melancholy — a little man who would never know serenity: only Happiness when he was doing pushups and Despair when he rested.

There is nothing in either the photographs or the

recollections to indicate that Eddie Slovik understood —
or perhaps even knew — that on November 7, 1942,
his fellow Americans were approaching the beaches of
Oran and Casablanca to begin the invasion of North
Africa.

3

The next twelve months, for Eddie and Antoinette
Slovik, were, for the most part, wonderfully happy ones.
Much of this happiness was derived from acquisition:
they both felt a terrible urgency about acquiring things
— the things everybody else has. So they both worked;
they both struggled to get raises in pay; and they were
miserable only when Antoinette was sick and couldn't
work, or when Eddie thought he wasn't earning enough
— when it seemed that they were not acquiring things
fast enough.

Their first acquisition was a bedroom suite, described
by Antoinette as "straight-lined, modernistic, blond
mahogany. . . . All our furniture was this kind . . . the
kind you see in ads in exclusive magazines . . . the kind
you see in the movies." They bought this the week they
were married, with money they had received as wedding gifts. They moved it into their first private apartment: two basement rooms next door to the Wisniewskis
in a house owned by a friendly couple named "Al and
Lela."

"Al and Lela were our first landlords," Antoinette said.

"They were a wonderful, middle-aged couple. We played cards with them several nights out of every month, either in their apartment or in ours; we were always getting together for a bite and a chat. We were very fond of them. Our apartment, as we fixed it up, became a cozy, two-room place — a big bedroom into which we moved our bedroom suite, and a kitchen and sitting room combined."

But Eddie had at least one attack of his miseries shortly after they had moved into this apartment. He recalls it in a letter from Camp Wolters:

I was thinking tonight of the times I caused you trouble during all our happiness. After we were married, remember at Lela's I wanted to leave you and you fought to hold me. You fought so hard that you were shaking. Forgive me, darling, for making you mad and miserable. Yes, I loved you at the time but it just seemed that I wasn't getting anywhere fast enough and I thought if I left, you might be happier. You know we had a tough pull on our hands when we were at Lela's. We tried so hard to get where we could have everything we needed, and, darling, I couldn't do it on $40 a week. I guess you knew that and I knew it, too. I didn't want you to go on suffering with me in that basement. That was no place for a loving wife like you to be. But you fought hard to hold me and after we finished painting and cleaned it up and got our dining room suit in it, it looked real cosy. From then on I wanted to move some place where we could be in heaven and we did. Then they had to take me away from all that and you. Oh, mommy, why did they have to do this to us? We were headed for happiness. Nothing was going to stop us. All we needed was a home and a new car. . . . I just pray the dear Lord that he will send me back so we can start where we left off when they did this to us.

It was after this realization that he had to earn more than his $1.05 an hour at Montella's that Eddie obtained the best job of his brief career. Entirely on his own he went to DeSoto, told the personnel manager his story, and was offered a job as a shipping clerk at a starting wage of $1.40 an hour. The parole officer approved the change, and he worked satisfactorily at DeSoto until he was inducted into the army in January, 1944.

The automobile was purchased a few weeks after the wedding: a second-hand Pontiac on which they made monthly payments. Eddie, however, could not obtain a driver's license during his two-year probationary period, so Antoinette kept the car and often picked him up at the DeSoto plant. He recalled this in another letter:

Gee, mommy, I need your home cooking. Remember when I use to work nites and you would pick me up from work and you had my favorite dinner ready for me, sour kraut and spare ribs. I wish I had a dish of it now 'cause I am so hungry. Remember them Sat. and Sun. nites when we didn't have any place to go and we would stay home and make love. We always did like that, didn't we?

The dining-room furniture was acquired eight months after the wedding. "It came as a surprise," Antoinette said. "On June 7, 1943, my husband took me out to dinner, and when we returned I could hardly recognize my own apartment. The Penn Furniture Store had delivered the dining-room suite while we were out, and Al and Lela had helped them place it. This was just one of the many wonderful surprises I had from my husband. Roses, jewelry, cosmetics — when he came home I never knew what the surprise might be."

During 1943 Antoinette lost only about two months' salary through being unable to work. She suffered no epileptic seizures, but she did have the first of her miscarriages: the other came three months after Eddie's induction. Their happy lives revolved around the basement apartment, their jobs, their plans, the Carmen, and Nick's Place.

"The Carmen Theater, on Schaefer Road, was within walking distance of our apartment, and we usually saw each change of feature, which was twice or three times a week. It was not a large theater, but it held so many memories for us. It is still there. And after taking in a movie we would end up at Nick's, a small restaurant operated by a Greek couple. The food was good and reasonable enough so that we could afford frequent visits. A hamburger, a cup of coffee, and we would head for home. Nick's was just a block from the theater, but Nick is no longer in business."

In the fall of 1943 Eddie and Antoinette made their biggest acquisition: they leased the upstairs of the duplex at 6320 Ternes Street — rental thirty-eight dollars a month — and they purchased living-room and kitchen furniture — payments seventy dollars a month — to match their bedroom and dining-room furniture.

They had not been following too closely the progress of the Second World War, but, like many Americans, they had their own private war plans: while the boom lasted they wanted to get as much as they could as fast as they could. They wanted to get all their furniture paid for, their car paid for, and by the time the boom ended, they wanted to have in hand at least the down payment on a home.

By November 7, 1943, their moving day and their first wedding anniversary, the Second World War was far advanced. Many of the climactic battles had been fought: North Africa, Sicily, Salerno, Stalingrad. Mac-Arthur was pushing toward the Philippines. Mussolini had been unhorsed. The massive air assault on Germany had begun. For anyone who wanted to make the most of that particular war, it was, indeed, time to get moving.

Here are Antoinette's recollections of that day:

—— At 6 A.M. the alarm clock chimed and we were both on our feet. Today was our anniversary. November 7, 1943. Our first anniversary. A very special day in more ways than one. Today we were moving out of the basement and into our new apartment. The upstairs of a duplex. We hurried into our clothes, and had breakfast for the last time in this little two-room place we had fixed up and shared for a year.

—— By 9 A.M. the moving van was at the door, and we were soon on our way. At the new apartment we unloaded the van, and then the second van arrived: the one from Penn Furniture Store bringing all the new living-room and kitchen furniture. By noon we had everything in the new apartment, and we started putting it in order. We were so happy we worked furiously, stopping only to congratulate ourselves and admire what we were doing.

—— Our living room was our pride and joy. Eleven feet by fifteen, with four big windows, and a door in the middle opening onto a sun porch. And every stick of the furniture new and modern and blond and straight-lined — just like we had seen in the movies. There was a dining room almost as big, and our furniture fitted it perfectly. The kitchen was beautiful, with a lot of light; the bathroom was perfect; and our bedroom was located in the rear, with another door opening onto another sun porch. This porch was not as large as the one in front, but on it Eddie would sit by the hour and feed his pet sparrows.

—— Our payment schedule was heavy: thirty-eight dollars a month for rent, seventy dollars on the furniture, sixteen-seventy-five on the Pontiac. But we wanted to pay for everything as fast as possible so that we could start saving toward a down payment on a home of our own. We had our hands full, but we loved every minute of our struggle.

—— About 7 P.M. that night I was scrambling some eggs for me and Eddie in the new kitchen. We were too tired to go out. My sister Helen came in. We both rushed out to try to show her everything at once. But she had a letter that had come for Eddie that afternoon at the old address. He took it and tore it open. And I'll never forget the look on that poor kid's face. He was stunned. He couldn't speak. He just handed me the letter while tears came into his eyes. The United States was considering changing his classification from 4–F to 1–A, and he was directed to appear for a physical.

—— We all just sat there in silence for a few minutes, wiping tears out of our eyes. Then Eddie said: "Wouldn't you know that they'd wait until a time like this! Eighteen months ago when I got out of jail and had nothing, they wanted no part of me! Now, when I'm a married man, with a pregnant wife, and *all this* — now they want me to go to the army! Wouldn't you know it!"

Four . . .

Wʜʏ had the United States changed its mind about Eddie Slovik? How is the mind of a nation, the will of one hundred and fifty million people determined and executed in such cases?

The will of a so-called free nation like the United States is determined and executed by many different agencies and persons. Sometimes the community will can be what a policeman says it is. Sometimes it's what a tax collector says it is. Or what the head of a senatorial investigating committee says it is. Or what the President says it is. Or what the nine members of the Supreme Court say it is. In the army much of the power of the United States — the power to inconvenience you, up to taking your life — is in the hands of a sergeant, or a captain, or a general, or a supreme commander, or the joint chiefs of staff.

Community power has often been galling to individual men. It can be an aggravation, an invasion of privacy, a damn nuisance. Community power, because of its tendency to arrogance, must always be suspect among free men. Free men create community power fearfully: there was not a patriot at Philadelphia who didn't fear the United States even while he was helping create it. Free men submit to community power reluctantly; they sometimes live to regret both creation and submission; and they follow this old, despondent course, not because they are unaware of its probable direction, but because they know nothing better to do. They are communal beings; they have primeval yearnings for the ant hill. For protection, perhaps, the community appears desirable or necessary; then it must be policed, defended, financed, expanded; there comes a class, rapidly proliferating, which finds purpose, not in the development of their individual personalities, but in "community work"; these communists exalt the community and low-rate the individual; until, finally, the individual loses the will or the opportunity to strive for individuality, he accepts commonness as a virtue and seeks it, he allows himself to be valued only in terms of service to the commune, and he finds community power no longer subject to his challenge.

This tortured twentieth century, already proclaimed the Century of the Common Man, is the century of the overexalted community, the overvalued group movement. Its wars are between these overextended complexes. Its "battles" are campaigns fought more by machines than men, decided more by logistics than individual exploit. Victory may be sought only to restrain or destroy rival community power, not to curb community power itself. So even if one is fortunate enough to be a citizen of the United States, where the individual is comparatively "free" of community power, victory may mean only a bigger state, a smaller soldier.

This is why the United States, in the Second War, had to hire the professors to devise orientation courses to explain to the individual why he should allow the community to inconvenience him. And this is why, in the case of *The United States vs. Private Slovik*, the burden of proof was, is, and must be — now more than ever — on the United States. For no matter how weak Slovik was, or how perverse, or how cussed, he was an individual; and in times like these, when the state waxes and the individual wanes, any challenge of community power by an individual should attract the inquiry of other individual men, hopeful of being able to lend their support.

This is not to deny the United States the right to inconvenience Slovik, even to kill him. It is not to say that wars should not be fought, or that the United States is not still worth dying for. It is not to question that grand objectives, including survival, may not still be achieved by resolute, flag-led, community action. It is only to remember that the United States was created and has been sustained by men who honestly feared it, for the purpose of making men free to be different, free to be weak, free to be perverse, free to be cussed, free to resent and challenge community demands on their private lives.

Mid-war, the United States changed its mind about Eddie Slovik. At the beginning, in his words, it had wanted no part of him; it had excused him from community service, allowed him extraordinary opportunity for acquisition. Then, suddenly, it canceled his immunity, destroyed his physical home, deprived him of his precious acquisition, and, when he resisted, demanded and claimed his life.

Why had the United States thus changed its mind? Did the community interest justify such a change? Was the change of mind a wise decision on the part of the United States? Was it fair to Slovik? Or is it possible that, in this manner in which he was drafted, Slovik was inconvenienced to the point of injustice?

2

From 1941 to 1945 the United States waged war on every continent, in every climate, with every known military weapon. It was called an "all-out" war against the slave principle. The United States organized and equipped the world's largest air force, the world's largest navy, partially equipped the Russian army and air force, along with the British and French, and organized and equipped a great mass army of its own.

The manpower, other than the professional military, divided somewhat in this manner:

At the top was the most fortunate group, the men with a wide range of choice, who were commissioned directly from private life. These were the professional men, the educated men, the men of position, the proud inheritors, the responsible custodians.

Then came the preferred services: the navy and air force. They took a very large share of the cream at all levels. They were not necessarily safer, but they were cleaner, more comfortable.

The army had a reservoir of good men from the regulars, the National Guard, the college training programs; and these became commissioned or noncommissioned officers and formed the backbones of the fighting divisions, or else were assigned to instruction.

It was a technicians' war, and the Seabees, the army engineers, the air force engineers — all of them competed for those Americans with skilled hands: plumbers, carpenters, electricians, mechanics, etc. These men got high ratings and high pay, and served in comparative safety.

Of the unskilled youngsters the Marine Corps had first choice. It could accept a volunteer at seventeen, so the Corps systematically combed the country for a million "combative types" — the boys who wanted to fight, who were, in fact, afraid the war would end before they could eviscerate some villain.

Whom did this leave for "dogfaces"? Whom did it leave for foot-slogging infantry privates in the last months of the war? Whom did it leave for the lowliest, loneliest role of all: the *replacement* private, the man who would be trained with one group, shipped with another, assigned to a replacement depot, then led to the front one night and told to dig in, without catching the name of his outfit, without knowing even the names of the men on his right or his left?

Obviously, for replacement infantry in 1944, the United States was employing those citizens who had no choice at all: the very young who had waited for the draft, the older or married men, or the marginal men who had been passed over, who had not been wanted, but who now were summoned by the community, most reluctantly, only when the barrel was being scraped.

The barrel-scraping began late in 1943 after one development and one decision.

The development was this: the United States was getting distressingly little mileage out of an infantry private. The Japanese, the Chinese, the Russians, the Germans — all of them had much cheaper, more durable models. The American infantry private was enormously expensive: he cost the taxpayer thousands of dollars by the time he was trained, equipped, paid, insured, entertained, medicated, educated, pensioned — almost as much as a small tank — and he wasn't lasting as long as the charts said he would. He got killed, or wounded, or sick, or he cracked up, or ran off . . . . So more replacements were needed . . . and *fast!*

The decision was this: despite all our sea, air, and possibly atomic power, it was decided to stage mass infantry assaults, not only on Fortress Europe, but also on the main islands of Japan. This meant a wheatlike sea of dogfaces, floods of replacements — so the heat was put on the draft boards: scrape the barrel . . . relax requirements . . . don't examine his eyes, count them . . . fill the pipelines so that dogfaces can be funneled into the lines in Europe in August, 1944, and in Japan in November, 1945.

—— We might take a million casualties in Japan!

This answers the question why the United States changed its mind about Eddie Slovik. Sure, he was a poor bet, but the United States was taking poor bets. The barrel was being scraped: he was one of the scrapings.

Did the community interest justify this change of mind? Who can maintain now that it did not? The men who were duly authorized to express the will of the United States insisted that it did.

The decision to assault both Germany and Japan with infantry was challenged by able Americans. Their argument was that Japan could be forced to surrender with air, sea, and atomic power; that the power of Germany, too, could be broken in this manner; that for the United

States to try to match its enemies man for man with bayonets was an indefensible waste.

The decision overruling this argument appears not to have been brilliant. But it was made in good faith by men chosen by democratic process to execute the community will in such matters.

Was the change of mind a wise decision on the part of the United States? It didn't prove wise in Slovik's case: the investment in him was a total loss.

Was it fair to Slovik? It would have been fairer for the nation to have drafted him when he first came out of jail, while he was still single, before he made down payments on living-room furniture. It would have been more considerate to have trained him as a member of a team, and sent him into action with buddies, with a platoon leader who knew how to reach out and catch him by the hand. But wartime limitations on national consideration for the individual are conceded by all thoughtful men.

In the manner in which he was drafted, was Slovik inconvenienced to the point of injustice?

In first classifying him as unwanted — in 4–F — then drafting him, the United States had been inconsiderate of Eddie Slovik. But inconsideration is not injustice.

Five . . .

BETWEEN November 7, 1943, when he received his notice of change of classification, and January 24, 1944, when he left for Fort Sheridan, Illinois, Eddie and Antoinette Slovik tried to enjoy their new apartment, worked as hard as they could and made payments in advance on their acquisitions, clung to one another, and sought consolation in the hope that either something would happen to prevent their being separated or that any separation would be brief.

The official *Order To Report For Induction* reached them on December 22nd — the day Eddie brought in the Christmas tree. The order was from Local Board No. 3, Wayne County, Fifth Floor, Cadillac Square Building, Detroit. It read:

The President of the United States,
To: Edward Donald Slovik
Order No. S-3281-A
Greeting:
Having submitted yourself to a local board composed of your neighbors for the purpose of determining your avail-

ability for training and service in the land or naval forces of the United States, you are hereby notified that you have now been selected for training and service therein.

You will therefore report at 3162 East Jefferson at 10 a. m. on January 3, 1944. You will there be examined, and, if accepted for training and service, you will then be inducted into the land or naval forces.

Signed: F. W. Price

They stayed at home Christmas, went nowhere, talked, figured. Neither of them could tolerate the thought of giving up their home: they had fought to get it, they were going to fight to keep it. Eddie's allotment payment to Antoinette would be fifty-five dollars a month. The payments on the furniture were seventy dollars a month. Then there were the rent, the car, everything else. And Antoinette was pregnant.

Could she hold up, stay at work, preserve all the gains? Or would the pressure and the worry bring on the epileptic seizures, weaken her so she couldn't walk, make her a liability instead of an asset?

And Eddie? He and Antoinette formed a team which, in fair weather, could survive, acquire, be happy, be good citizens. But could he be a good citizen if he became frightened, if he felt he was losing, if he was forced to assume new responsibilities alone?

On January 24, 1944, Antoinette and her mother drove him to the New York Central station in Detroit and told him goodbye.

[63]

From the time he entered the service until his execution on January 31, 1945 — 372 days — he wrote Antoinette 376 letters. Most of these were written from Camp Wolters, near Mineral Wells, Texas, where he took his basic training. All but a few were written before August 25, 1944, the date of his alleged first desertion. He often wrote her as many as four letters a day; and these letters, considering that they were written hurriedly, in pencil, usually while he sat or lay on a cot, with other men around, are quite legible, neat, the spelling is good.

These letters should be preserved in the Library of Congress, for henceforth they must be required reading for any scholar who would understand the Second World War. They are the anguished outpourings of a man who thought of himself as America's most inconvenienced individual; they are the war diary of America's most distinctive soldier.

Here are the most meaningful excerpts, interspersed with explanatory comment and reports from Antoinette:

Fort Sheridan, Jan. 26, 1944. Mommy, I am lost without you. . . . I think I'm going to have a lot of trouble. Army life don't agree with me. . . . Last night I couldn't sleep. . . . I'd rather be home digging ditches. . . . Please don't cry; I know you cried last night. . . . I'm so lonesome.

Jan. 28. I got my insurance policy. It's for $10,000 at $6.70

a month. That's quite a bit of money, but I can make out somehow. . . . I know you are lonesome, but believe me I'm worse off than you.

Camp Wolters, Jan. 31. Mommy, I just arrived in Camp Wolters, and is it warm. I left Fort Sheridan Saturday night and arrived here Monday afternoon. When we stopped in Moberly, Mo., the American Legion was out there and treated us with coffee and doughnuts, and I thought it was nice of them to come out on Sunday and treat us. I sent you a telegram just as soon as I got here. . . . I also sent you some handkerchiefs. I am in the infantry for 17 weeks and after that I don't know where I am going. . . . This camp is nice, but this what you call 3.2 beer really stinks. . . . Honest, honey, I feel like crying every time I sit down to write you a letter. . . . I am so unlucky.

Feb. 1. Everybody has to have 17 weeks of infantry; that's what we call basic training. I also had what you call KP. . . . Darling, don't think I was bad to get KP. You see we have so many men in our company and each one has a try at it. They drop our names in a box, and the ones they pull out get KP for that day. . . . I also had my first training in arms. I learned how to clean and take a rifle apart, and I learned all about booby traps.

Feb. 2. This army life doesn't give you time to do anything for yourself. . . . You have to be on the jump all the time. . . . You know what I feel like doing, don't you? I don't have to tell you . . . but I'll try my best. . . . The name of the town we are near is Mineral Wells, Texas. You can find it on the map and you'll see just how far I am from you.

Feb. 3. Just to try to call you up today I had to miss one of our classes, and I'll have to take punishment of some kind tomorrow.

Feb. 5. Darling, every time I see another fellow and his wife around camp, it chokes me.

Feb. 6. Honey, remember that last day we were together, and how I got up from bed and see you laying there, and how I just had to cry? Sometimes now when I read your letters and think how hard it is there by yourself, I just have to cry. . . . Prove to your sisters that you can get along and that you don't have to worry cause I'll be home. . . . It's Sunday and I don't have my pass to go to town, but I don't care. How in the hell can a guy go to town without his wife?

Feb. 6. Did you get my insurance policy? I pray you'll never have to use it. . . . The people here in Texas are pretty mean; they only look out for themselves.

Feb. 6. This is the third letter I have written you today. It's the only way I can feel close to you.

Feb. 7. Honey, let's pray the baby looks like me. I think it will. If anything happens to you, I'll go AWOL, and that's just what I feel like doing now. This joint is worse than a rat hole. The food is terrible; the work is tough. But I'll get back to you no matter what happens. . . . Did you get the four letters I wrote you Sunday?

Feb. 7. I have to run down to the hospital tonight. One

of the fellows is sick, and he wants me to bring him some stuff.

In the army Private Slovik earned the same reputation he had at Ionia: he was a good buddy . . . do anything in the world for you. . . . A goodhearted fellow . . . do anything I told him to do. . . . A damn good guy: I liked him a lot.

Feb. 8. Today we were out for reveille. The band was out there, too. We had to salute the flags. It was swell. Gee, honey, I wish you was here to see it. I know it would make you cry because it almost made me cry.

This is one of three references in the letters to patriotic emotion. Nowhere is there a single mention of Adolf Hitler, or of war aims, or of the desirability of victory, or of the progress of the war. His letters during the week following June 7, 1944, contain no reference to the D-day landing in France. But apparently he was not completely impervious to the army's efforts to bring him to think more about the flag and less about his own problems.

Feb. 9. I just read Helen's letter [Antoinette's sister] and she wants to know are there any pretty girls down here and how come I'm not in the air corps.

Feb. 10. Darling, the fellows are razzing me cause I write so much. They say what's the use of writing so much for your wife's already running around with some other John. But I know different.

Feb. 10. Honey, we had a course in gas. We had to go through a chamber of gas with our gas masks on. It was awful. One of the gases made us take our rings off, and that was the first time since we've been married that I had to take my ring off. I hated to do that but I had to. I was thinking of you and it sure made me sick to take it off. . . . I wrote a letter this morning and the sergeant gave me hell because I wasn't supposed to write in the morning. . . . The way I feel I don't care if they kick me out of this dam army. I'm failing in all my lessons. I'm not thinking of the lessons, just about my wife. You can't blame me, mommy, can you? They treat us like a bunch of kids. That's all there is here, just kids, I'm an old man. This noon I had to carry a fellow to the hospital because he broke a leg. They make you jump over high objects that you can't reach on your toes. Honest, honey, I don't like it here. . . . It's just like being in jail. Only in jail it isn't this bad. I don't think I'll even get to be a corporal. I don't care.

Feb. 11. I haven't anything to say this morning except that this joint makes me sick. It reminds me of jail cause thats just the way they treat us. You can't do this and you can't do that cause they'll throw you in the guard-house.

Feb. 13. When I think of the swell times we had to-gether, mommy, it makes me mad. I can't understand why they did this to us. . . . I'll be home soon. I know I will. I'm not trying to learn anything cause if you're too smart

[68   ]

or too good they'll send you overseas. I'm sure you don't want that to happen to me, do you dear?

Feb. 13. Save everything for me, mommy, and be sure to save a soft shoulder for me to cry on, cause I'm really going to cry when I get home. This place is just about killing me. . . . I'm so lonesome I could scream out loud. . . . Honey, if anything happened to you I'd just have to kill myself or start to steal again.

Feb. 13. Mommy, I just can't see why they did this to you and me. We love one another too much to be separated like this. We haven't done anything to anyone to have to be separated like this. If we were mean to each other there would be a reason for it. Darling, why couldn't they leave us alone? I could scream.

Feb. 14. When I go to bed at night I'm just lost. I haven't got anybody to warm their feet when I get in bed. Remember, darling, how close we used to sleep together? I cry almost every night.

Feb. 15. There have been many nights that I spent awake just thinking about you with somebody else . . . the fellows rase me and paint awful pictures of you in bed with some other guy. . . . Please mommy try to help me forget such awful things.

Feb. 14. Today is Valentine's day, and I miss you awful. I went to town yesterday and got you a nice Valentine's card. It will be late getting to you, but honey they didn't have any cards here in camp, and I had to go to town to buy you one.

Feb. 16. I'll never come back to Texas as long as I live. I think it stinks. I hate this place more every day. I had three shots in my arm and my sore tooth pulled today.

Feb. 17. I have just gotten back from a hike and believe me I'm tired. I had my rifle and a fifty-pound pack on my back. Gee, honey, they try to kill the fellows here. It's one of the toughest camps in the union. . . . When I'm on a hike, dear, I can see you on the highest mountain top and some of the mountains here are pretty high. Gee, honey, I wish you could see Texas. It's beautiful, the grass is green, the sand is bright red and the rocks are pretty. The colors blend in so nice. Honey, you should see the cactus — they're nice and green. It's pretty all except the work. . . . Today, dear, I was out on the firing range learning how to shoot. I'm trying to act just as dum as I can cause the smarter you are the faster you have to go overseas.

Feb. 18. Today is my birthday, mommy, and I received the wrist watch you sent me.

Along with the watch Antoinette sent a letter from which this is an excerpt:

Feb. 18. Happy birthday, daddy, and that comes from the bottom of my heart. I love you, dear, and it just doesn't seem right that we had to be torn apart. Darling, I just got through eating my lunch, and oh! how I wished you had been here to enjoy the lunch with me. I was planning too much, I guess, that's why they took you away from me. But, daddy, you are going to be home soon, aren't you?

About the wrist watch Antoinette recalls: "On his

[70   ]

birthday, February 18, 1944, I bought him a Gruen Curvex wrist watch. I paid sixty dollars for it. On the back of the watch I had his name and date of birth engraved. I was able to buy him the watch because I was still working at that time. That watch was his most prized possession. I wonder what became of it?"

The Seibold Hotel, Fort Worth, Texas, Feb. 20. Honey, I have just gotten my weekend pass and I am at the hotel named above. I have two other fellows with me. Darling, please don't think I am cheating on you cause I am not. I did have a couple of beers but the beer here is 3.2. I am just going to have some whisky and coke and I am going to get good and drunk. I don't care if they have to carry me out of this hotel. We bought a pint of whisky for $6. Pretty high, don't you think? I'm a little tight, but don't worry honey, I still love you. . . . Your soldier husband.

Camp Wolters, Feb. 21. I got back from town Sun. nite. I had a swell time. When I got to the hotel I got good and drunk and went to sleep. I didn't get up until 10:30 Sun. morning. It was sure a releaf to get away from camp, but when I seen all them other soldiers walking around town with their wives and girl friends I just about burst out in tears.

Feb. 22. Darlin, I am blind without you. You were the light in my life. It was you that put me on my feet. It was you that made a man out of me. Without you I'd probably be an ex-con all my life. I'd probably still be in jail. That was one reason why I married you cause I knew you was

[71   ]

just the type of woman that could straighten me out. Remember how you tried to get rid of me. I wouldn't let you go cause I had found the one I needed most. . . . I tried hard to win you and I think I did a pretty good job. Honest, mommy, it was hard to get you. It was worse than standing up next to a guy and fighting to win. Darling, you looked so pretty, and when you tell me how you are dressed in your letters I can just see you and I feel like crying but I can't cause the other fellows are here. But when I sleep I always cry for you. . . . As you can see, mommy, I stole some paper from that hotel that I was staying at over the weekend. . . . Your blue-eyed daddy.

Feb. 24. You are sick, darling, but what am I going to do? . . . I am going on the rifle range Sat. and I am going to foul up. I'll try to have a poor score so they won't send me overseas. If I am dum on everything they might send me home cause I won't be able to fight. . . . The other day we went on a hike and one of the fellows passed out. They work the guys until they fall out, then they just dig a hole and throw him in. Oh, darling, I don't know what to do to be with you again. I am so dam sick and tired of this place I feel like going AWOL. I'm sorry I didn't go to jail for six months then I know you could come to see me any time you wanted to. Aren't you sorry that I didn't go to jail instead? After my six months was up I wouldn't had to go to the army at all. I could be with you now, dear. This way I don't know when I will ever see you again.

Antoinette's tribulations had begun, and Eddie had learned about them, not from her, but from a friend.

[72]

She had had her second miscarriage, after which the epileptic seizures began again.

"I had as many as seven strokes of epilepsy in one day," she recalls. "I couldn't go to work, and with all the new worries confronting me for survival, I began to have more difficulty walking. My whole body seemed paralyzed at times. My doctor urged me to undergo surgery, but I didn't have the money. Even if I had sold everything Eddie and I owned, I still wouldn't have had enough money for hospitalization. As a final stroke of bad luck, my eyesight started to fail. After trying to help myself, I asked the Red Cross for aid and got the cold shoulder. I went on living in misery — ill health, no job, debts, nothing but Eddie's fifty-five dollars a month — trying to hold things together. My mother, as the final act of her life, tried to come to my rescue. She gave me massages and hot baths, and gradually I began to feel better. I tried to keep all this from Eddie, but he could call the switchboard operator where I had worked and she would tell him the truth."

Eddie's writing that he was sorry he hadn't gone back to jail indicates that he, no doubt, considered this course when his classification was changed. He still had six months of probationary time hanging over him, and he could have escaped the army with a simple parole violation. He could have got drunk, or disturbed the peace, or banged into a parked car and been caught without a driver's license, and he would have gone back to Ionia for six months.

In December, 1944, locked up in the Caserne Mortier in Paris, his life in Eisenhower's hands, Eddie was to recall bitterly how easily he could have escaped by following such a course.

Feb. 26. Gee, honey, my ears are ringing. I just got off the rifle range. You know how I use to jump when I heard a little noise. . . . Tonite I went to the beer garden and had three bottles of beer and a box of cheese-its. You know how I use to eat cheese-its when I was home. Well, tonite I ate the whole box all by myself. . . . Mommy, I never found any fault with you. I never said anything about your leg. You were never a cripple to me.

Feb. 27. Mommy, you try to be a good soldier. I make a poor soldier, but I want you to be the sargent and I'll be the private. You give me the orders and I'll listen. . . . I miss your home-made cakes and pies and I miss the fruit you always had on the dish for me. I miss the good coffee you make, and, most of all, I miss sleeping with you.

Feb. 27. Darling, remember when you sent me that wrist watch. I cried like a baby. I could kick myself in the pants when I think of the times I mistreated you. How mean I was to you at times. Once I wouldn't talk to you for almost a whole day. And how hard you tried to make me smile when I was mad. I never knew that I could be so happy with you, mommy, until it was too late. . . . I have quite a few friends here and they all hate the Army just like I do. I don't blame them any.

[74]

Feb. 28. I just got off the rifle range and my ears are still ringing so my writing is very poor cause I am nervous. . . . Mommy you said you were down to the Red Cross and you want me to go to my commanding officer. I'll try and see him tomorrow. I'll let you know in my next letter what he said. Keep your fingers crossed. You know what my chances are in anything. I always have the bad luck, and I'll probably have bad luck in trying to get a discharge. You know, honey, that everything happens to me. I never get a break. But, mommy, I'll see him tomorrow and see what he has to say.

Feb. 29. Darling, I tried to see my CO but he was on a furlough so I'll have to wait until he comes back. I'll try my best, mommy, to get a discharge, but I don't think I can make it cause it's a little too late. You try and see what you can do.

"Yes," Antoinette recalls, "I tried to get him a dependency discharge. His commanding officer wrote me what to do. I obtained letters from physicians who had attended me. One of these was a doctor of physiotherapy who had treated me for about six years while I was in school: otherwise I wouldn't have been able to attend school at all in my early years. I got several letters of personal reference, a statement of financial condition, and a letter from my employer. All these were sent to Eddie and he turned them over to his commanding officer. Action was slow, and then a Red Cross representative called on me — a woman, strictly out for blood.

"After talking with this woman, I could tell from her words and actions that she wasn't interested in my welfare. Her suggestion was that I not pay all the rent, and thus have more money left from the allotment for food. When I asked her what I would do when I got notice to move, she calmly told me to dispose of my furniture and move into one room, or go to my family or Eddie's family to live.

" 'This is wartime,' she said. 'We all have to make sacrifices.'

" 'But what will my husband have to come back to?' I asked her. 'Can you imagine what this apartment means to my husband — a boy who never had a home and who spent five years in jail? Can you imagine what this furniture means to him and me? How much we worked to make the payments on it?'

"She didn't like what I said to her, and when she left she said it would depend entirely on Eddie's commanding officer whether he got to come home or not. That wasn't true, because Eddie was a favorite of his commanding officer, and the officer told Eddie that if his discharge depended on him Eddie could be home in twenty-four hours. I know what sort of report that woman sent in.

"When things got real tough, I tried everything, and got doors slammed in my face. I tried the draft board, the Social Welfare, the Red Cross again, and, as a final resort, I wrote a letter to President Roosevelt. I told him the whole story. I got a letter acknowledging receipt, and my hopes were renewed. But it was all in vain. At this point I gave up hope: I just prayed to God that some miracle would happen to bring him back, to save our home, and put me back on my feet."

March 1. Mommy, I just got off the rifle range and my score was bad but I don't care. When I got down there to shoot I was scared. I tried to tell them that I was nervous but they made me shoot anyway. Everytime I would shoot I would close my eyes and jump and when I would do that I would miss my target. You should have seen my score. I am going up again for three more days. Then I have to shoot for record. I don't think I'll pass and I don't care. I'm not trying to be a good soldier. I want a discharge and if I don't get home soon I'll go crazy. Mommy you are the only one I can depend on. You know my mother would not send me anything and I would starve before I would ask her.

March 2. Gee, mommy, I need your home cooking. . . . I just got off the rifle range and my cheek is big. Everytime I shoot my rifle it jumps and kicks me in the cheek. But I guess the swelling will go down in a couple of days. My score is pretty bad, I don't think I'll make it. You don't mind if my score is bad, do you mommy? You'll still love me, won't you?

March 2. I'm getting fat, mommy. I weigh 145. . . . I haven't told you this before cause you said you were jealous. We have quite a bit of Wacs down here. But don't worry, mommy, I'll never cheat on you cause I love you too much.

[77]

March 3. I just got off the rifle range and my cheek is worse than yesterday. I had such a bad score that they made me shoot all over and now it makes six days that I have been shooting and my arm is sore and my cheek is swollen. Some of the fellows got black eyes and some got their lips cut. Anyway I wasn't any good so I have to shoot all over again. . . . One of the fellows had a quart of whisky last night and I got drunk again. That's the only thing I have to take my mind off this camp.

March 4. I just got off the range and I was a bolo. I didn't make the score so I have to go again Sunday. I'm sick and tired of shooting my rifle.

March 4. Please don't worry so much about our baby cause it's only meant for us not to have one now. . . . Some day we're going to have one of the cutest babies in the world. And don't tell me that cute is bollegged.

March 5. Honey, I know you're doing a lot of crying. Did you ever see a good soldier cry? You told me you'd be a good soldier and keep your chin up.

Antoinette denies that she ever wrote Eddie any sad letters. "I wrote him as many as four letters a day," she says, "but I tried not to let the troubles show. When I took ill and didn't have anything else to do, I whiled away my lonesome hours writing to him. I wrote him one letter twenty-seven pages long. I painted a vivid picture for him of our love nest. If I rearranged the furniture, I would draw him a plan so he could see it better. He used to like to watch me dress, so I described in detail how I was dressing, step by step. I wrote not only letters; it was more like a story. He lived from one mail call to another; and if the mail was delayed he worried. He lived only for me, and I lived only for him."

March 5. I just got back from supper and they didn't have anything to eat as usual. The food is cold and it isn't cooked the way I like my cooking done. I can't get used to eating this trash. Remember how I use to tell you how they fed us in jail? Well, it's worse here. . . . After supper I was down to the service club and I had some ice cream but I couldn't stay there cause there are a lot of soldiers with their wives and I got so lonesome I had to come back and write you again. Oh, mommy, how much longer is this going to be? . . . I had to cheat to make a score of 140 points on the rifle range. But I made it. So I guess I'm in the army, dear. But please don't worry. I'll be home very soon. The CO is back from his furlough and I'll try to see him. It's pretty hard to talk with him but I'll try. Me and a couple of fellows bought a quart of whisky. Maybe I can get sick enough to get a discharge.

This reference to cheating on the rifle range reveals an interesting characteristic of Slovik's. Apparently he'd go to the range scared and determined to foul up. Then what Napoleon called the "fear of invidious distinction" would start working on him — not much, but a little. He'd somehow get by, and then be almost proud to report to "mommy" that he had passed.

[79]

March 6. Mommy, the CO got back and I had a talk with him and as far as I know I think I'll be home soon. Soon as I can have the Red Cross sign some papers. I'm supposed to go down and see him tomorrow morning and when I do it will have to be up to you and your doctors and the Red Cross to get things straightened out so be careful what you say and how you say it. . . . He asked me how come I didn't try to get a deferment when I was home and I told him I was supposed to get a deferment from the factory but my boss was in the hospital and when I got my induction papers it was too late to file for a deferment. I'm supposed to fill out some sort of papers and then send them to you and you are to take them to the Red Cross and have them signed. I'll let you know tomorrow night so just keep your fingers crossed. Please, mommy, try your best and see what you can do at home when I send those papers.

March 7. I was down to see the CO this morning and I couldn't do a thing. He told me before he could do anything he had to have three affidavits and a Red Cross report. You need money to have things done like that. If I was home I probably could get it. You do the best you can, mommy. . . . You said something about my parole officer sending you a card about me making my report. Well, yes, I was supposed to let him know that I was inducted. Well, I didn't let him know. I wanted him to look me up and throw me in jail. I'd have been better off. They may still throw me in jail; I hope they do. I can always find a way of getting out of jail but I can't find a way of getting out of here. I guess I'd do anything to get out of here, darling. Oh, mommy, I guess our hopes of me coming home to you now are spoiled.

It was at this point that Antoinette was visited by the Red Cross woman who advised her to give up the apartment. And here is further proof that Eddie had been tempted to try to return to Ionia before his induction. He had deliberately failed to make his regular monthly report to his parole officer, hoping that this failure to report would constitute a violation of his parole and cause him to be returned to jail for six months.

March 9. Darling, you know that the only reason I let you work when I was home was cause there was so many things we needed. I'm glad, mommy, that you did work. You know how tough it was when you wasn't working. If you didn't work to help me out we wouldn't have all that pretty furniture you have, darling. You have one of the prettiest homes in Dearborn. It isn't quite completed but it will be when I come home. That's why, mommy, I hope you can keep working for a while till we get everything we dreamed of. . . . Darling, try your best to keep your chin up and be a good soldier even if I aint. . . . You know your dreams are just like mine. A big house nice furniture a big car the best that money can buy. Our dream of having a baby around the house, mommy, that's all we want. That's why I wanted you to work to help me out. Don't fall down on the job now, mommy. . . . As for the baby don't worry so much about it. When I get home I'll take you to the best doctor and find out why we can't have any. I'll find out whether its you or me, it might be me. . . . Forgive me for not writing to you yesterday. We went out on a 18-mile hike last night, and I was so dam tired, mommy. I walked so much that my little toe was bleeding. Some of the fel-

[81   ]

lows fell out. . . . I'll walk, mommy, until I drop dead. I told them about my toe bleeding but they said not to worry and they didn't do a thing about it. They don't care. . . . I had my examination for overseas duty the other day. We all had it. The kind of examination they give you you couldn't fail. You could be dead and they'd say you were alright.

March 9. Darling, why didn't you tell me sooner about your fainting spells?

March 10. After I got off the rifle range I'm feeling pretty good. Don't worry about my cheek it's in good shape now. My little toe is getting along okay. But I have to go on the rifle range again. I'll tell you how I make out. They had me at the eye clinic and they wanted me to wear glasses but I told them I wouldn't wear them. So they said if I don't want to wear them then it's no use wasting the governments money. I don't think I need them do I dear. . . . I'm glad to know that you are getting the bills paid. I always want my bills paid.

March 13. I didn't do much on the rifle range. I boloed again. I couldn't even hit the darn dummy. They have dummy japs for us to shoot at and fight with. At the end of our rifle we have a ten-inch knife that we are supposed to use to cut up the dummys with. I don't like that. I can't hold my wind when we run or go on a long hike, mommy. I run out of wind and my side bothers me but I don't complain to them. It don't do no good. They only put you in the guardhouse or on KP or make you work on Sunday. I'm beginning to hate this place so much I'm almost crazy.

I worry about you so much that I'm losing my hair. I'll be bald-headed when I get home.

March 14. Mommy, if only they knew what they are doing to both of us they'd send me home.

March 18. All I eat here, darling, is candy.

March 24. I finished firing the machine gun and I had a pretty good score. But I hate guns.

March 25. Oh my darling I need you to mend my socks, iron my shirts, wash my clothes, and cook me something to eat. . . . Tomorrow morning I'm going over to unit #2 with those papers you sent me. Oh my darling mommy if they turn me down I don't know what I'm going to do. I think I'll die. . . . I was down to headquarters this morning with those papers and they asked me a lot of questions about you I couldn't even answer but I did my best. He wrote a statement and they'll send it to my commanding officer. Let's keep our fingers crossed.

March 27. I know mommy that I can't spell or write. I'm just a dum Polack. . . . I never did know anything. Today my CO called me out to sign a statement. I had three papers to sign. I signed them but that's all I did. He didn't say anything but I tried to read as much as I could on them and I think it's my discharge. . . . They'll probably send you to the Red Cross for examination and then it's up to you.

March 29. Darling, I haven't heard anything from my CO yet. Have you heard anything about my discharge?

March 31. Darling, we had to get our rifle cleaned up for inspection and it took us all night to do. We had to go on the rifle range this morning and shoot at moving targets and you know how much I hate to use a rifle. Tomorrow morning we have to fire the machine gun and when we get through we have to clean them. . . . You can be proud to say that you have a husband in the infantry because it's one of the toughest jobs in the service.

April 1. Just when I had everything I had dreamed of, they have got to take me away from it. When I was in jail I dreamed of you and everything we have. . . . Now I can just lie here and see my dreams go up in smoke, and I want to cry. Why do they make us suffer so? Why do they hate us?

As you read Private Slovik's letters, you find yourself wishing that, just once, he'd try to define the word "they." But he never does. And in the last minutes before the volley that ended his life, he was still using they. Since the execution order was issued by General Eisenhower "for the United States," *they* is the community, the United States.

April 2. Remember darling when I said we were up for examination. Well they put me in class 1-a. That means I'm fit for overseas duty. I wouldn't mind it if I could just know that I was coming back.

April 2. Every time I go to the show here at camp I try to imagine I'm at the Carmen. . . . I try to make you a good husband. I don't fight with you and get drunk and beat you up, and I never will. I've seen so many homes broken up that way, and I don't want our heavenhome broken up. You know how my mother and dad got along when they would drink. I'm also glad darling that you don't drink. . . . Please go to the Red Cross again. I can hardly wait for my discharge. . . . But if you must know I don't think it will work. They need quite a lot of fellows for overseas duty and I think I'm one of them. . . . I'm sorry darling that I ever made you work. I guess I was selfish for money. After I had been in jail, and you know how it was at home, I wanted money to buy all the things that other people had. You know dear how mad it made me feel when I seen somebody else have something that we didn't have. It still makes me mad darling. . . . I'm glad I won you and have you for keeps. . . . I won that fight to get you, but now I'm in a spot where I'm helpless. They've got me; and even if I tried I doubt if I could win cause the odds are so against me.

April 3. I just got your letter saying your sister is spending the weekend with you. I only wish it was me instead of her. But you didn't let her sleep on my side of the bed did you darling. I hate to have anybody — even your sister — sleep in my place. Please mommy you sleep on my side and let her sleep on your side.

April 4. They had a examination again and I didn't go cause I'm sick and tired of examinations. The way I feel now mommy I could die. Or even go AWOL. Some day I might.

April 5. Oh mommy when are they going to send me back home to you.

April 7. Must run now mommy. You see we have shows that are just for armed service men. They names of them are why we fight the enemy and we must see them.

April 10. This will be a short letter for I have that speed hike to make today. We got eight miles in one hour and 50 minutes. That's about a mile every 15 minutes. Last time we had four miles in 50 minutes and I almost passed out so I don't think I'll make this one tonite. But I'll try my best. So far I've been doing purty good and I don't want to fail now.

April 11. Well darling I made that speed hike and I feel swell this morning.

At this point it appeared almost as if Private Slovik was going to make a soldier. The program was ingenious and effective. It was designed to wrench a boy away from his home environment, then keep him so busy that he wouldn't have time to think about homes and girls and wives and mothers. Normally, around the eighth or ninth week, a trainee began to respond to his heavy-caloried diet of fight films, fight talks, speed hikes, obstacle courses, firing, grenading, bayoneting, constant appeals to his competitive instincts, flags, bands, marching-in-step. He began to feel rugged, prideful, combative; and his home and his women faded far enough back into his memory so that they didn't interfere with his soldiering.

In Slovik's letters you can watch the tonic working. It *almost* made a soldier of him. The army almost won its bet on him. But just as Harry Dimmick and Ionia hadn't gotten him until he was eighteen, the army hadn't gotten him until he was twenty-four.

April 13. Darling I have to go on the range again and learn how to fire a 60 mm mortar. We have so many different kinds of guns to fire that I know that if I told you the names of them you wouldn't know what they are so I don't bother.

April 15. Darling I was down to company headquarters to find out about those discharge papers and he said that it takes quite a bit of time for them to okay it. You see darling they don't care much about giving me a discharge. They take their sweet old time. Why should they worry about you and me mommy. Some of the fellows say it takes from 8 to 10 months.

April 15. Remember that letter you said you was going to send me to show my company commander. Well dear I'm not even going to open it. I'm going to send it back home to you. Really darling I'm afraid to open it and read it. It'll have so much in it about your troubles, and you know how that's going to make me feel. So I'd rather not touch it. So I'll send it back to you and you send it to my CO. Write to First Lt. A. Shaw, company commander, 59th Infantry Training Brigade. I really don't want to read it dear. If you do write to him let me know so in case he does call me out I'll know what to say to him. It's really hard for me to get to talk to him but I think he's a nice fellow. In fact we all think he's swell and nice to talk to but we hardly get a chance to talk to him. Darling I hope you can understand why I don't want to read that letter. You have so many troubles . . . but I have more troubles than you.

April 16. Darling those bed of roses I have built around you have to be taken care of. They need water on them every day just like I need you every day. Darling without water on those roses they will die. Without you and your love I will die. So we are just like a couple of red roses deeply in love with each other. Darling without each other and our love we will bend and die. . . . I miss you in all your beautiful surroundings. I miss watching you getting dressed to go out with me.

April 20. We have a parade march today. Gee I wish you was here to see the parade. It's purty. . . . I'm always on edge cause I think they will call me out and give me that discharge any day now.

April 21. I got back from Dry Valley this morning at 2:30 a. m. I didn't get to sleep till 4. Yes, darling, I could tell you an awful lot about Dry Valley, Hells Bottom, Barkers Hollow and many other places, but I don't want to worry you.

April 21. Mommy I just got back from that examination and I don't have to tell you what happened. The kind of examination they give you here don't mean a thing. Why a little baby could give you the same kind of examination. They ask you how you feel and you tell 'em okay and they say alright that's all. . . . If I have to stay here much longer I'm afraid they won't send me home at all. What am I going to do?. . . We have a big beer party at 5:30; I guess I'll go. I didn't go the last time cause I stayed in and wrote you a letter. Don't worry darling, there won't be any women over there, just soldiers. They throw three beer parties for us during our basic training and this is the second one. I pray darling I'm not here for the third. The only party I want is one with you. . . . The fellows rase me about all that lipstick you put on your letters. I just tell them that it goes to show my wife loves me. . . . I have to go on the rifle range and fire again. You don't know how much I hate it.

April 21. I'm going for another classification again today. You see we have three of them to go thru. I'll pass I guess.

April 23. Please mommy let me know if you hear anything from the Red Cross. There's nothing I can do here. It's up to the Red Cross now. If they say it's okay then I'll be home. Otherwise I'll never see you again.

April 26. I won't be back till Sat. morning. We have a 26-mile hike Friday from Pinto Ridge. It will take us about eight hours. Remember that last 18-mile hike I took my toes started to bleed. Well mommy what's going to happen to me when I take this 26-mile hike?

April 29. Gee mommy I just got back from Pinto Ridge and believe me it was tough going. We had to sleep outside on the ground and eat outside in that sand and walk 26 miles and are my feet sore. The food was terrible. We had to get up at four oclock in the morning and eat breakfast and it was dark and we didn't know what we was eating. All we had for breakfast was half a hot dog half a bowl of mother's oats with no milk, a cup of coffee and half a orange and we were still hungry. Then we put our tents up and fired the machine gun for two days. Darling you just don't know how mad and sore I was and still am. We still have three more weeks like that to go. All they have here is snakes, bugs, skunks, worms and big jack rabbits. We couldn't even have a good nights sleep we were so afraid of them snakes. On that 26-mile hike we had to walk up and down steep hills over rocks and over soft sand like they have on a desert. And the hell is just starting. Monday we leave for Dry Valley and we won't be back till Saturday.

April 29. Mommy why did they have to do this to us? We were headed for love and happiness. All we needed was a home and a new car. I just pray the dear Lord that he will send me back so we can start where we left off when they did this to us. . . . Darling you go right ahead and sleep with my picture on your breast. You think you are silly for sleeping with my picture and sleeping on my side of the bed and drinking out of my cup since I been gone. But I love you when you are silly. Don't stop being silly.

April 29. Yes mommy I'll keep that date with you at the Carmen and then we'll go to Checkers Inn for a beer. . . . My CO should have heard from you by now. If he calls me out I'll tell him everything I can. . . . But what are we going to do if they don't give me a discharge. I guess I'll just kill myself. I always have my rifle here at my bed and it wouldn't take much. I'm sorry darling that I mentioned that but I love you so much I'm crazy. . . . What will you do now during these days when I can't write. I want you to sit in my chair in the front room with your feet on that footstool and reread my letters and think of me out there in Dry Valley and on Pinto Ridge with them dam snakes. And when you start to cry just close your eyes and relax and think of me. And then read some more of my letters.

April 30. I went to church today and prayed for them . . . that they would send me home. . . . I'm enclosing a couple of mother's day cards for Holy Mass on the 14th of May. Please give one to your mother and one to yourself. The reason I'm sending you one is cause you are my mommy and I have to think of my darling mommy. But I pray that I'm home in your arms before the 14th of May.

May 1. Darling I'm off to Pinto Ridge and Hell's Bottom and Dry Valley, and I won't be able to write to you.

May 5. I wish they'd make up their minds what they're going to do with me. . . . The Red Cross man says they're not giving out any more discharges, but that they will give you the operation on your leg. I want you to go down to their main office and talk with them. Go even if you have to take a taxi.

May 5. I went down last night to see my CO but he wasn't in. The fellow that was in charge told me that he sent you a letter telling you what you should do to get my discharge. Well he let me read the copy of the letter he sent you but darling from what I read it don't mean a darn thing. Cause mommy we did all that already. We got all our papers signed and the doctors signed and I signed the discharge paper like he told you I should do. From what I gather he can't do anything till he hears from some other headquarters over here. I was going to go down there this morning, but I'll have to wait till I come back from more maneuvers. Meantime darling you go down to the red cross chapter and see if you can't do something.

May 15. I read in your letter that the woman from the red cross was over to see you again. I know how mad you must have been when she told you that they haven't done anything about my discharge. . . . When I get back from Hell's Bottom I'll do everything I can to get out of here.

May 23. Dear the other fellows are getting ready to ship out on their furloughs and then they'll be sent overseas. My furlough papers haven't come yet, so I'm working hard on that discharge.

May 24. The fellows call me the great lover because I get so much mail. They just don't believe you'd write me five letters in one day.

May 24. There was a fellow here who got a discharge and he waited nine months. I'd sure hate to have to wait nine months. I went down to the red cross and all they could say was sorry Slovik we can't do anything till we hear from your CO. So I'm trying to see him now. It's getting pretty hard to get hold of him but he's a nice fellow. . . . Darling the fellow from the red cross said they'd have to get an okay from my draft board. You said you was down to see them. What did they have to say? Please see if you can't make an appointment with them and have a good hard talk with them. Then they in turn will notify the IRTC headquarters here. I can't even get in that headquarters. The red cross over here is really swell and they got the letter from red cross headquarters in Detroit and he said I have a good chance of getting a discharge if they will work on my case. He said that headquarters have asked them for a letter bearing on my case but that that was as far as they've gone with it. He said honey that as far as he knows they might have my letter in the drawer and forgotten all about it. Why do they treat people like us this way?

May 24. The fellow from the red cross said that one reason why I didn't get my furlough papers may be that they were trying to make up their minds whether I'm to get a discharge or not.

May 26. Dear I was picked to go Sunday to Ranger, Texas, for a military funeral. Its given by the American Legion. Its about 80 miles from here. Gee I sure wish you was there watching me honey. Its an honor to go there and I was one of six soldiers picked to go. One of the major's friends died and he wants us for his funeral. . . . I have a picture of the whole platoon but I can't send it home cause I'm afraid it might crack all up.

May 27. Darling today was graduation day for our basic

[93   ]

training. The band played while the major made a speech and we had a big dinner — no beer. It was swell. Darling we won the gold cup for having the best company in camp and that means a lot not so much to us but to the CO. He's really a nice guy.

Here is Slovik's most engaging characteristic. With everyone in authority he knew his relations were cordial. This is what Harry Dimmick meant when he said he wasn't a cop-hater. Slovik always thought his officers were nice guys — even including the provost marshal who gave the command to fire on him — and they thought he was a goodhearted kid. But, at the same time, Slovik felt that *they* were always out to get him; and *they* did get him. If only Slovik could have ever known them . . . and *they* could have known him.

May 28. I was over to Ranger, Texas, today for that military funeral and oh honey gee I wish you was there to see it. It really upset me to see all those graves and the mothers and wives with their little babies crying. It upset me so dear that I was weak in the legs. I was really shaking and nervous. I pray darling that you won't ever have to put flowers on my grave. . . . But gee mommy were the people ever so swell to us over there. It never cost a cent. They bought all our eats drinks and smokes. I went to church over there and the people invited us over to their house for dinner. Really darling I thought it was nice of them. The Chief of Police drove us to church and said if we were in town again he would be glad to give us anything we wanted. We couldn't walk two blocks without somebody stopping us and shaking our hands and asking us over for dinner or for a drive around town. It really was nice and I had a swell time.

June 12. Gee honey I hated to do it but I had to wire you for $35 to come on my furlough. I hope you can get it. I asked the red·cross for it but they won't give it to you unless its an emergency furlough. All I'm waiting for now is some money so I can come home.

June 13. While I was writing to you last nite mommy Western Union called me and said I was to hurry down and get the money you sent me. I was so happy to hear from you dear and get the money. But I won't be home until about next week. Don't worry I took the money you sent me and put it in the bank until I'm ready to come home.

Antoinette recalls: "I got the thirty-five dollars from my mother. She was over at my apartment massaging my legs when the letter came asking for it. While Eddie was home on his ten-day furlough, he did some plumbing work for a friend, and with what he earned he repaid mother."

June 14. Everything is going to be alright, mommy. I'm sure I won't have to go overseas and I'll be home Saturday.

June 15. I go for my examination this afternoon. So far I'm in Call 1-a, and they always ship the 1-as first, that's why I'm so sure I'll be home next week.

June 15. I know mommy you haven't got any money. What are you going to do, dear. I hate to have you sell your wrist watch. I could have sold my watch for $50 but I knew it came from your heart and darling I wouldn't sell your heart. Oh my darling what are we going to do. I don't want you to have to go hungry or to have to beg for food. I know where you got the money you sent me. Its the money you had saved up for the rent. Oh mommy how are you going to pay the rent. I don't want you to sleep out in the street. Why must they treat you so mean. I can take a lot of punishment and it wouldn't bother me. Its not me I'm thinking of. I never was any good and I guess I never will be. Its you I'm so worried about.

June 21. I've signed my furlough papers, but every time I think I'm about ready to come home they turn me down.

June 26. I didn't write for the past few days. I suppose you know by now. I was planning on coming home by the first of July, so I thought I wouldn't write cause I'd be home before you got my mail. But darling as you can see I'm writing to you again because I won't be home by July 1st. They are keeping me here for some unknown reason.

June 27. Darling they can't seem to make up their minds as to ship me as yet. They won't ship me overseas so that's one thing you won't have to worry about.

June 28. Darling you won't have to worry about me ever going overseas cause from the way things look now here they may not even give me a furlough, cause they don't know what to do with me.

This was the cruelest period of all on Private Slovik. His buddies — the company which had won the gold cup — all left on their furloughs, then reported to embarkation points and went overseas. But not Slovik. For seven or eight weeks after he had completed his basic training, he was kept on at Camp Wolters, idle, cutting grass, pulling guard duty, watching a new wave of trainees, mostly eighteen-year-olds, begin their routine.

Just why he was held up can't be established now. Perhaps someone along the line was actually considering giving him a discharge. The best guess is that he was still the sort of guy who gets moved only when the barrel is scraped: no regimental commander seeking replacements, shuffling through the cards of that training company, would have chosen Slovik. Eddie would move only when some colonel was forced to accept him in a two-out-of-three deal: we'll let you have those two probable scrappers, Colonel, if you'll take this one probable washout.

It's at this point that Eddie's letters start coming hard. He has nothing to offer each day except a new excuse for his furlough's delay . . . a new theory about what they are going to do with him.

July 4. Oh mommy darling I do hope they make up their dam minds as to what they intend to do with me. I'm getting awfully sick and tired of having to hang around here and just waiting and wondering what they are going

[97   ]

to do. All I'm doing now is pulling guard every other day. In other words I'm just a gold brick in the army.

July 5. In a way I'm glad darling that I'm still here cause the longer I stay here the more delay it gives me from going overseas. The fellows that finished their training with me, well 80 per cent of them are overseas already. I got a couple of letters from the fellows overseas and they said they like it better then over here in Camp Wolters. I believe them dear cause this is really a tough place to do your training in.

July 7. Darling I would have written earlier this morning but I was busy scrubbing the floor for the fellows. I didn't have to do it but they are on the rifle range and I know just how tired they get so I thought I'd do it for them.

Here is Private Slovik, the good Samaritan, again. On November 12, 1944, the day after he was sentenced to death at Rotgen, Germany, he was the prisoner who swept out the guardhouse so that the other guys, who had gotten only twenty years, could sleep. His jailer said: "You had to like the little sonofabitch; he'd do anything in the world for you."

July 7. Mommy I'm awfully fond of you this morning, but I have to tell you that there isn't much of my life left to live. My life is short and you have made it sweet. By the first of August I'll be overseas. But I'm going to die and you'll marry some other man. Before I die I'll whisper mommy darling I love you. When I'm on my furlough it'll be the last time I'll ever see you again. I'll only pray that you can find a man who'll love you like I did and who will treat you as good as I tried to.

Private Slovik arrived in Detroit on his furlough July 12, 1944, and was there until July 23rd. Except when he was doing the plumbing work in order to get money to pay for his transportation, he spent virtually every hour with Antoinette. They went to the Carmen; they had beers at Nick's; they stayed at home with their precious furniture. Eddie sat on the little sun porch out back and tried to pet a new generation of sparrows. But there wasn't much gaiety; he couldn't push himself up to much Happiness.

Antoinette had pawned her watch for money for Carmen tickets and beer and sauerkraut and spareribs. She hadn't worked since February. The Penn Furniture Store was worried about the delinquent payments. The landlord wanted the rent caught up. Eddie, for the first time, and the hard way, learned about epilepsy. He learned that his wife, whom he had thought of as so strong, was, indeed, a cripple.

When he left for Fort Meade, Maryland, the money in his pocket had come from Antoinette's rings going into the pawn shop.

Fort Meade, July 24. It seems, mommy, that ever since I was born I've had hard luck. I spent five years in jail, got

[99   ]

out when I was 22, got married when I was 22, lived 15 months with my darling wife and was so happy with her, and now they break up my happiness, put me in the army, and try to kill us both and take everything we've got. Oh mommy dear why don't they leave us alone. We didn't do anything to anyone did we?

July 27. We are going out on maneuvers and believe me it's tough. The whole place is rough and tough. I wish I was back in Texas. We will get our new rifles tonite and I guess we will have to take them right with us.

July 28. You said it was up to me dear to get out of the army. . . . Well if you knew how hard it is to get out of the infantry you wouldn't ask me to.

July 28. Oh mommy we've had a hell of a time here in the past two days. They just worked us to death. We went out last night and crawled on our stomachs for about 65 yards with machine guns firing over our heads and explosives blowing up in front of us. We didn't get to sleep until 1 a. m., and we had to get up at 5:30 for house-to-house firing and close combat firing. Gee mommy I'm sure glad that's over with.

July 29. Darling I would have talked longer on the phone last night but I started to cry and in another minute I would have bust out in tears. . . . I have all my clothes packed and ready to ship. I'll leave Monday. I'll be in Company A, 4th Platoon, I don't know what that means but I hope its for the best. . . . Darling the only way you can get out of this army now is to have two glass eyes. Just one won't do any good.

[100   ]

July 29 (Saturday). All the fellows are going to town for their last time cause they won't be here Monday. I sure wish I could go with them darling. But if I did go I wouldn't be able to write to you, so I would rather stay here in camp and write and talk to you on the phone.

July 30 (Sunday afternoon). I went to church this morning and I went to confession and holy communion and the priest really gave me hell. At first I was kinda scared to go because I knew he would give me hell. Maybe its good he did. . . . Mommy remember when I was home and you and me was playing with the weegie board. We asked it when the war would be over and it said on September 7th. Well dear the paper today said the same thing. They expect the war in Europe to be over the 7th of September.

July 30 (Sunday evening). I'm sitting here now thinking how good your voice sounded to me over the phone a few minutes ago. We talked 12 minutes and it cost me $3.69. I almost fell over when she told me what the bill was. But darling I don't mind . . . honest I don't dear. After I got thru talking to you I went over to the PX and got some pop and gum. I got eight packages of gum at three cents a pack. I sure needed it cause I was out. [This was their last telephone conversation.]

Camp Kilmer, New Jersey, Aug. 1. Well honey from here on somebody else will be reading my letters and you know how I hate to have somebody else read my mail beside you. But whoever reads it doesn't know me or you so what difference does it make. We're not overseas yet.

Aug. 3. Gee honey they make me so dam mad that I'm on the urge to do most anything. I can't see how anybody can be so mean. Here they take an honest man and put him in service and treat them like a bunch of dogs. Its just like a barking dog. He'll take so much till he's hurt and then he'll bite. But I guess they don't care.

Aug. 6 (Sunday). Darling from where I am sitting I can see New York. I can see the Empire State Bldg. In the dark it's a pretty thing to see. . . . Its our life we're losing and they won't let us do what we want with it. Every time they want something done we're right there. But when we want something done, they treat us like dogs. The trouble with the people back home is that they think a soldier's life is a life of roses.

It is ironic that Slovik embarked from Camp Kilmer. For he was destined to sleep the long sleep in the same cemetery as Joyce Kilmer: Fère-en-Tardenois — the only difference being that Kilmer lies in the honored area, while Slovik lies in the camouflaged, dishonored back yard.

Just after dawn next day, August 7, 1944, through the early morning mist, the old *Aquitania* pushed off from a New Jersey pier, with seven thousand dogface replacements packed in her like sardines. They were heading for Britain and Normandy; and, while Fate hadn't yet cast the dice, Private Slovik was heading for the 109th Infantry Regiment, the 28th Division.

For that date, August 7, 1944, the official history of the 28th contains this entry:

On this date, at Gathemo, the division fought its bloodiest battle of the Northern France campaign. In the initial phase of the attack the 109th was hit extremely hard with artillery and small arms fire. . . . At 2100 all battalions were ordered to dig in. Before a satisfactory position could be established, the Germans launched a heavy tank counterattack which struck the entire 109th, especially the 2nd Battalion, a hard blow. . . . Three German tanks accompanied by more than 100 infantrymen moved east along the highway which marked the left boundary of the 109th. The tanks turned up a trail leading into the flank of the 2nd and 3rd Battalions, and suddenly switched on powerful searchlights which illuminated the area where our men were digging in. The tanks opened up with machine guns and 88's at ranges of 50 to 75 yards, while, at the same time the German infantrymen opened fire with a large number of automatic weapons. The 109th took very heavy casualties; and only the magnificent courage of our bazooka men, themselves taking the cruelest casualties, beat off the German tanks and prevented a greater disaster.

That was Private Slovik's outfit. They were waiting for him. They needed many replacements.

Six . . .

IF BETWEEN 1864 and 1953 the United States was to shoot *one* citizen soldier for cowardice, it is logical that the shooting should have been done, for the United States, by the 28th Division — Pennsylvania National Guard — and by its 109th Infantry Regiment. The 109th, which comes from Scranton, has this motto: LET THE CITIZENS BEAR ARMS.

No unit bearing arms for this community of free men is older or has a prouder heritage. As part of its treatment for combat fatigue during the Second War, the 28th required its faint-hearted men to read and recite the division history. Private Slovik never knew this history. The replacement system and his own weakness or perversity denied him a chance to know it. Perhaps he might have acted differently had he known it.

The 28th's first elements were organized by Benjamin Franklin before the Revolution. Three companies served in the Continental Army — as General Washington's bodyguard. Then there were the War of 1812, the Mexican War . . . all the wars — even the Philippine Insurrection and the Mexican Border. . . . Some element of the 28th has drawn blood and given blood in every war in which the United States has been engaged.

On the field at Gettysburg, high up on Missionary Ridge, there is a monument marking the crest of Pickett's Charge. The inscription: THE HIGH WATER MARK OF THE CONFEDERACY. That was the point of deepest penetration by the South, of gravest danger to the Union. And the men who held that position for the United States — who beat back the last, desperate thrusts of courageous enemies — were of the Philadelphia Brigade . . . the 28th Division.

In France, near the village of St. Agnan, department of the Aisne, not far from where Private Slovik is buried, there is another "high-water mark." It is the point of furthest penetration of the last, desperate German offensive of July, 1918. There, for three days, another Cause hung in the balance. Little, frightened men stood fast in the mud and died while, far away, in safety, their fellow inheritors of freedom waited for the enemy to be repelled. Those men who held that position for the United States, who slew the flower of the kaiser's army and piled them up like cordwood — they, too, were of the 28th Division. Pershing called them the Iron Division; the Germans in both wars called them the *Blutig Eimer*, the Bloody Bucket —

from their red keystone shoulder patch and from the quality of their soldiering.

At one point in the Meuse-Argonne offensive in the First War, a battalion of the 109th Regiment was commanded by a sergeant: all the officers were dead or wounded. And, strangely, within four hundred yards of Slovik's grave, in 1918, G Company of the 109th, the company with which Slovik was either unwilling or unable to stand, came out of a fight with only sixty of its two hundred and forty men still on their feet.

In four and a half months of combat in France, 1918, the 28th lost 14,139 men, of whom 2874 were battle deaths. From August, 1944, to August, 1945, in France, Belgium, Luxemburg, and Germany, the 28th took 26,286 casualties, of which 3266 were battle deaths. The authorized division strength in the Second War was 14,243.

In the Second War, too, there was another of those last, desperate lunges by the enemy — the Ardennes counteroffensive, the Battle of the Bulge — and the 28th was there. But this time their job was not to stand at the high-water mark, but to slow the attack, to roll with the first punch.

At 5:30 A.M. on December 16, 1944, the 28th was "resting" and reorganizing, training replacements, in Luxemburg, holding a twenty-five-mile front — a normal front for a corps. Division headquarters was at Wiltz; Clervaux was the recreation center, with many officers and men relaxing there — fishing, going to movies, drinking beer. Suddenly these recreationists were blasted out of their bunks by von Rundstedt's barrage; and, pouring through that loosely held front, came elements of the nine best divisions Hitler had left. The 28th was supposed to disintegrate, and by nightfall of the first day the Germans were scheduled to have taken Bastogne.

The hitch in the German schedule came when the 28th did not disintegrate. On its left flank the inexperienced 106th Division did shatter, but two regiments of the 28th held together and fought while falling back. The 109th Regiment killed two thousand Germans in one afternoon. Platoons, companies, battalions were pocketed time and again, but kept fighting. The cooks at division headquarters turned riflemen. The division bandsmen, some of whom had played with the Dorsey brothers and Artie Shaw, turned grenadiers after losing their instruments. Then, too, a good many men, officers included, threw down their equipment and ran like those scared rabbits.

Incredibly, the whole Allied front had been taken by surprise, and in a sterner day some general, perhaps even Eisenhower, might have been relieved and court-martialed for it. It was a greater tragedy than Pearl Harbor, could easily have been forestalled, should have been anticipated. But such mistakes are tolerated in the higher echelons; and maybe it has always been this way. The Light Brigade charged at Balaklava only because some general had fouled up, and Tennyson reports no court-martial.

At any rate, to discharge their responsibility to the United States, the men of the 28th Division had to fight for time: time for Patton to ram into the German flank with his tanks, time for the 101th Airborne Division to dig in at Bastogne, time for Eisenhower to re-order his chessboard. And this time — four precious days of it — the 28th Division bought with skill, courage, and blood.

A correspondent for North American Newspaper Alliance wrote:

Now that the von Rundstedt counter-offensive has been stopped, it is only fair that the people of the United States know that the 28th Division deserves equal credit with the gallant men of the 101st Airborne at Bastogne for stopping this German drive. Three days before the 101st began its stand, the men of the 28th were taking the full brunt of this mighty German effort, fighting desperately in hundreds of scattered battles, outnumbered eight to one. The soldiers of today's 28th have proved themselves worthy heirs of fathers who stood at Gettysburg and St. Agnan.

But it was this faculty for attracting the onslaught of five enemy divisions that earned the 28th the Second War reputation of being a "jinxed" or " hard luck" outfit. Ernest Hemingway in his *Across the River and into the Trees* has his tired old warrior comment:

"Jesus, Daughter," he said. "You've got an awful lot of problems on your hands. The next thing, they will parade the twenty-eighth division through."

"I don't care."

"I do."

"Were they not good?"

"Sure. They had fine commanders, too. But they were National Guard and hard luck. What you call a T.S. division. Get your T.S. slip from the Chaplain."

And Churchill, in *Triumph and Tragedy*, writing of the Normandy campaign, says:

[The situation] . . . offered a tempting opportunity for a German attack striking westward from the neighborhood of Falaise. The idea caught Hitler's fancy, and . . . on August 7 [the day Slovik sailed from New York] five Panzer and two infantry divisions delivered a vehement attack. *The blow fell on a single U.S. division,* but it held firm and three others came to its aid. After five days of severe fighting . . . the whole salient from Falaise to Mortain, full of German troops, was at the mercy of converging attacks from three sides. The Germans held stubbornly on to the jaws of the gap . . . and no fewer than eight German divisions were annihilated. [Italics Huie's.]

It was slow, tough going, all through the war, for the 28th. They were held out of the fighting in North Africa, Sicily, and Italy. They had to train for three years, from February, 1941, when they were nationalized at Indiantown Gap, Pennsylvania, to July, 1944, when they arrived in Normandy. This meant they also functioned as a training organization for other divisions, frequently losing valued officers and men to other outfits. They trained in seven states — General Omar Bradley commanded them for a period — until they were moved to South Wales for six months more training, then to Devonshire for three months training in hedgerow and amphibious tactics.

Once in Normandy, they promptly got the hell shot out of them in the Falaise action, losing many fine non-coms and officers at the company and battalion levels. They had three different commanding generals in twelve hours: one CG was killed by a sniper just four hours after he had assumed command.

They were the American division selected to parade through Paris on August 29th: the full treatment, battle dress, a twenty-four-man battalion front, bands, flags, Arc de Triomphe, Place de la Concorde, Bradley and De Gaulle in the reviewing stand, all that stuff. But they were not given leave in Paris; just marched up to the Siegfried Line where they began the slow, bloody business of blasting dragons' teeth and those superpill-boxes. They were the first division to enter Germany; they put the TNT to one hundred forty-three of those superconcrete forts; and they lost plenty of good men doing it.

Then came the "Green Hell of Hürtgen." Hürtgen Forest. And now it was November, wintertime, and the infantryman was in his four elements: ice, mud, blood, and TNT. The Germans played their old game of ganging up on the 28th, and the result was what every commander dreads: static warfare. No progress, no getting on with it, you just lie in the mud and slug. You take a town today, lose it tomorrow, and bury your dead. This means casualties, despair, combat fatigue, and replacements, replacements, replacements. The replacements are green; they don't last long; they either get killed, wounded, sick, or they bug out; and this means more replacements.

After Hürtgen, for the 28th, came the Ardennes fight — the hell *really* shot out of them — with serious losses in killed, wounded, and prisoners. Then, in February, 1945, the last big action — reduction of the Colmar pocket: deep snow in the Vosges Mountains . . . using mules for supplies . . . driving the last Germans from French soil — the action in which the present junior senator from Michigan, Charles E. Potter, lost both his legs — the action in which the 109th Regiment won the Croix de Guerre.

That was the 28th Division, toward which Private Slovik was sailing during the second week of August, 1944. A big, tough, hard-luck, meat-grinding outfit that the people of the United States had organized, trained, equipped, paid, and sent to France for only one purpose: to kill Germans.

One night around August 11th or 12th, when the

Aquitania was in midocean, two privates lay in their narrow bunks far below decks cleaning their rifles. One of them was Eddie Slovik, and the other was his new buddy, also from Detroit, Private John P. Tankey.

"You know, Johnny," Slovik said, "I don't know why the hell I'm cleaning this rifle. I never intend to fire it."

Tankey replied: "You don't know what you'll do, Eddie. But you better be careful. You can get in trouble talking that way."

2

Just as the Slovik case brings distinction to one private soldier, to Ionia, and to the 28th Division, so it also brings further distinction to the two graduates of West Point who ordered and carried out the execution: Dwight D. Eisenhower and Norman D. "Dutch" Cota. Eisenhower made the final decision for the United States; Eisenhower *ordered* Slovik shot, he didn't simply "decline to intervene," as in the Rosenberg case — the legalities are not the same. Cota had convened the court-martial, approved the sentence, and then — on Eisenhower's order — it was Cota who stood in the snow, faced Slovik, saw him shot, and reported to Eisenhower that the order had been carried out.

The world knows Eisenhower: that is, the world *partially* knows Eisenhower. Much of the world doesn't know that the Eisenhower jaw, which falls so easily into

The Grin, can also slam shut as fiercely as a bulldog's. It was Eisenhower who gave Patton a chewing-out — a chewing-out so awesome that even today top sergeants from the old cavalry come to attention when they hear about it.

Relatively few Americans know Dutch Cota, but those who do will tell you that if, between 1864 and 1953, *one* West Pointer would have to stand up a private soldier and have him shot for "failing to perform his duty to the United States," then Dutch Cota was the man who could do it.

When General Cota stood there on January 31, 1945, in the snow, two stars and the American eagle visible on his battle dress, facing Private Slovik, who was bareheaded, an OD blanket around his shoulders, all insignia of the United States ripped from his uniform, there, for the world, was the perfect contrast between Weakness and Strength. For in the powerful, two-hundred-pound, fifty-one-year-old frame of Dutch Cota was imbedded all the strength that can come to a man from goodly heritage, strong environment, iron discipline, rigid education, and love of country. His folks had never had any money — rich men don't go to West Point: it's a "trade school" — but everything in Dutch Cota's life had equipped him to be the proud inheritor, the responsible custodian, the resolute defender of the faith.

He was born in Chelsea, Massachusetts; attended Worcester Academy. He is not German, as the nickname implies, but a mixture of old English and French Huguenot: an Episcopalian. His father was born in Vermont. At West Point he was Class of 1917, with classmates like "Lightning Joe" Collins, Matt Ridgeway, and Mark Clark.

To review General Cota's Second War record is to recall some of the finest hours of the United States Army. He fought in North Africa with the 1st Division, the 16th Regiment. If they aren't the best in the world, the United States can depend on them until the best arrive. They were also at Omaha Beach.

At Omaha Beach General Cota was assistant division commander of the 29th Division — Virginia and Maryland — the 116th Regiment. If someone hadn't thought they were the best, they wouldn't have been in there; for they had the job of blasting with "hand-placed charges" those hideous iron-and-concrete beach obstacles.

Most of us who were on that beach on the morning of June 6, 1944, are willing to concede that General Cota earned the Distinguished Service Cross he received from the United States. Hundreds of Americans died there that day — for the Cause of Liberation — and, but for Cota's skill and courage, many more would have died.

At 7 A.M., when he reached the low, rocky escarpment at the high-tide mark, the invasion force was a cold, wet, confused rabble, strung out for three miles, clinging to the rocks, getting the hell shot out of them.

Cota's judgment: "There are only two kinds of Americans on this beach: dead ones, and those who soon will be dead unless we move forward. So we move!" And the movement began — slow, tragic, heroic. One man crawling forward, clearing a mine, inching close enough to hurl a grenade into a pillbox, killing the enemy. The cry: "Knock 'em out, open the access roads, so our stuff can come through." General Cota personally directed the opening of two access roads, the killing of many enemies, while overhead his son, Lieutenant Norman D. Cota, Jr., also of West Point, flew a P-47 for the United States Air Force.

At Saint-Lô, still with the 29th, General Cota won the Silver Star for gallantry and the Purple Heart for wounds. His role, like that of his friend, Brigadier General Theodore Roosevelt, Jr., was not only to help direct the American effort, but also, through personal example, to try to inspirit Americans, to invite them to be courageous, to feel sure that they would win. It was leaders like Cota and Roosevelt who deliberately walked in the open, defying enemy fire, not to display reckless bravado, but to encourage Americans to come out of their holes, to charge forward, to understand that sometimes the best way to save your life — and your nation's life — is to charge the enemy, not wait for him.

After the 28th Division had been shot up at Gathemo, General Cota took command — August 13, 1944 — and he led them all the rest of the way: through the remainder of the Normandy fighting, at the Siegfried Line, in Bloody Hürtgen, at the stand in the Ardennes, at Colmar; he trained them for the assault on Japan, all the way down to inactivation at Camp Shelby, Mississippi, December 13, 1945. Now retired, he is an adopted Pennsylvanian: he lives in Bryn Mawr, Pennsylvania.

General Cota reminds you of a piece of good, solid, fine-tempered steel. White hair, gray eyes, inclined to corpulence, he is a modest, quiet man who can chuckle. He has none of Patton's belligerent swagger, but he is a soldier. He is everything that West Point strives to create: a reliable instrument for the preservation of the United States . . . a man who can fashion and use reliable instruments for the large-scale slaughter of this nation's enemies . . . an individual whose vocabulary has one key word: DUTY.

The second highest ranking combat officer standing in the snow, facing Private Slovik at his execution, was Lieutenant Colonel James E. Rudder, of Brady, Texas, commanding the 109th Regiment. He is a leaner, younger version of Cota. But he is not a West Pointer; he is a product of the school which supplies more infantry commanders than does West Point — Texas A & M. He had landed on D day as commander of two battalions of Rangers: specialists in assault. In this action he was wounded three times, refused evacuation, and was awarded the DSC.

Jim Rudder's attitudes are expressed in his message to his regiment on January 31, 1945:

MESSAGE

TO: Soldiers of the 109th Infantry

Today I had the most regrettable experience I have had since the war began. I saw a former soldier of the 109th Infantry, Private Eddie D. Slovik, shot to death by musketry by soldiers of this regiment. I pray that this man's death will be a lesson to each of us who have any doubt at any time about the price that we must pay to win this war. The person that is not willing to fight and die, if need be, for his country *has no right to life.* [Italics Huie's.]

According to record, this is the first time in eighty years of American history that any United States soldier has been shot to death by musketry for deserting his unit and his fellow man. There is only one reason for our being here and that is to eliminate the enemy that has brought the war about. There is only one way to eliminate the enemy and that is to close with him. Let's all get on with the job we were sent here to do in order that we may return home at the earliest possible moment.

JAMES E. RUDDER
Lt. Col., Infantry
Commanding

So there, on August 13, 1944, was the conflict. Private Slovik, despondent over his deprivations, yearning for his wife, his apartment, his Pontiac, his furniture — he was in midocean, cleaning his rifle, but determined that he would never fire it.

Waiting for Slovik in the Normandy hedgerows was the bloodied 28th Division, hard luck, with much killing yet to be done, and with traditions to uphold. And also waiting for Slovik were three soldiers — Eisenhower, Cota and Rudder — armed by the United States with the power of life and death over privates, and convinced of their soldiers' creed that *an able-bodied citizen who won't fight for his country doesn't deserve to live.*

Such a conflict, if maintained, could have only one final, logical conclusion. But thus far — since the Civil War — this conclusion had, somehow, been avoided.

Seven . . .

At this point, as a guide to the subsequent material, it is necessary to present the time schedule of the Slovik case.

On August 7, 1944, Private Slovik sailed from New York on the *Aquitania*.

On August 14th he landed at a Scottish port; was transported by train to Plymouth, England; was given two days' instruction in hedgerow fighting, then shipped to Omaha Beach, where he arrived on August 20th.

On August 25th, during the afternoon, Slovik was among a group of twelve replacements who, having been assigned to G Company, 109th Infantry, traveled by truck from the vicinity of Damville toward Elbeuf, in an effort to join the company. In this group, besides Slovik, was his buddy, Private Tankey, and a Private George F. Thompson, 35244119, whose address at that time was Route 1, Gary, Indiana, and who was a witness for the United States at the court-martial.

During the night of August 25th, at Elbeuf, Slovik

is alleged to have committed what is referred to as the First Desertion: he and Tankey never made physical contact with the company.

Between August 26th and October 5th, as soldiers lost or somehow separated from their outfits, Slovik and Tankey subsisted with the Canadian 13th Provost Corps.

On October 8th, near Rocherath, Belgium, Slovik and Tankey physically joined G Company, 109th Infantry, for the first time; and about an hour later, Slovik alone, with Tankey pleading with him not to do it, committed what is referred to as the Second Desertion.

On October 9th Slovik voluntarily surrendered to officers of the 28th Division, confessed to desertion, and was confined in the division stockade.

On October 19th charges were preferred; on October 24th charges were investigated; on October 26th Slovik was offered an unofficial deal by Lieutenant Colonel Henry P. Sommer, the division judge advocate, whereby he could escape court-martial by going into the line. Slovik refused the deal, and on October 29th his case was referred to trial.

On November 11th, Armistice Day, on the second floor of a public building in Rotgen, Germany, Slovik pleaded Not Guilty before a nine-officer court-martial presided over by Colonel Guy M. Williams, of Harrisburg, Pennsylvania, 28th Division finance officer. The sentence: death.

On November 14th Slovik was confined in the Seine Base Section stockade, Paris.

On November 27th, after conferring with Colonel Sommer, General Cota approved the sentence.

On December 9th Slovik addressed a letter to General Eisenhower, pleading for clemency.

From December 1, 1944, to January 6, 1945, the case was reviewed by seven Army lawyers in Paris, including the Army's foremost legal authority Brigadier General E. C. McNeil, who had handled clemency matters for General Pershing.

On December 23rd General Eisenhower confirmed the sentence.

On January 23, 1945, General Eisenhower ordered the execution, specifying that it be carried out in the 109th "regimental area."

On January 30th a four-man MP detail took Slovik from the Caserne Mortier in Paris — in a weapons carrier — and headed for the place of execution, St. Marie aux Mines, France. The detail was delayed by a heavy snowstorm and did not reach the place of execution until 7:30 A.M. the following day.

On January 31st, at 10:04 A.M., in a well-enclosed courtyard commandeered for the purpose, Slovik was shot before General Cota and forty-two selected witnesses. The highest-ranking witness after General Cota: Colonel Edward L. R. Elson, a chaplain, who, in 1953, was minister of the National Presbyterian Church,

Washington, D.C., the church to which both President Eisenhower and General McNeil belong.

2

During the sixty-day period from August 7th to October 8th, Slovik's constant companion was John Tankey, who now lives, with his wife, at 23520 Ann Arbor Trail, Dearborn, Michigan.

Tankey and Slovik had much in common: both Polish, both from Detroit, both had wives to whom they were devoted; Tankey had been a "crib man" at Chrysler, Slovik a shipping clerk at DeSoto. They had met at Camp Kilmer through being lined up in alphabetical order: Slovik, Tankey. . . . Where you from? . . . So am I. . . . From then on they're buddies . . . and during the six weeks they spent with the Canadian Provost Corps, they were a conspicuous Yank twosome, adventuring through France and Belgium.

Tankey, once he had "physically" joined G Company on October 8th, apparently made a good soldier. His explanation that he had "got lost" at Elbeuf was accepted, and he soldiered until November 5th, when he was seriously wounded by shrapnel in Hürtgen Forest. Thereafter, he was hospitalized in France and England until March, 1945. As a rifleman with a marksman rating, he received the ETO ribbon with three bronze stars, the Purple Heart, a Victory Medal, and a good-conduct ribbon.

After that afternoon of October 8th, when he had tried to persuade him not to take off, Tankey never saw Slovik again. He assumed, however, that he was all right, and knew nothing of his trial and execution until I gave him this information in September, 1953.

The information stunned Tankey. He couldn't eat; he was physically ill for two days; he couldn't believe it, kept shaking his head, saying that it was all wrong, that Eddie was a damn good guy.

Tankey is about five-eight-and-a-half, one hundred forty-five pounds — Slovik's size. He has brown hair, graying at the temples, a Fancy Dan brown mustache, blue eyes. On the day he was interviewed he was wearing a white shirt, green sweater, yellow-and-green bow tie, brown hound's-tooth check pants, and yellow-and-green argyle socks. He went back to Chrysler, has had some promotions, is now a "follow-up man" — speeds delivery of tools and machinery. Three years ago the leg in which he got the shrapnel was cut up again in a disastrous automobile accident: his wife lost a kneecap, his mother-in-law was killed.

Here is Tankey's account, interspersed with explanatory material:

—— Well, like I said, Eddie and me met there at Kilmer. We were there several days on an orientation deal: some colonel who had fought somewhere in the Pacific telling us, "War's no damn fun; some of you are going to get killed." Then we went to New York for embarkation on this boat. I thought Eddie was about like all the rest of us: he said the same things and seemed to feel about like the rest of us. We all looked at the Statue of Liberty as long as we could see it and wondered if we would ever see it again.

—— Eddie's bunk was right across from mine. He used to sit there and write letters to his wife. He was always writing home and showing everybody pictures of his wife. He was a good worker. He was good on KP, I remember. He was a swell guy. He was kind of serious. He always had a serious look about him. Kind of stern. If you didn't know him you might think he was mad. He was real sincere. He never had a smile, except maybe if he had a few drinks, or sometimes when he was talking about his wife. He talked a lot about his wife. He said his wife made a man of him, and he wished he had met her years before he did. He said the only time in his whole life when he felt happy was when he met her, and when he was courting her and they got married. He felt bad because he got drafted and he had just been married a short time and had to leave her. He was proud of her. He said she limped just a little. He showed her picture to everybody.

—— He told me how he was in trouble when he was a kid. He said he was in the Boys' Republic and in some kind of reform school. He never went into detail about what kind of trouble or anything.

—— Like I say, I thought he was a swell guy. He

[124   ]

never talked about deserting, no. And he sure didn't ever seem to me like a guy that was yellow. We got put way down below decks going over. The boat traveled in a zigzag line to avoid subs. Once I remember we could hear shooting above decks. Some of the guys got kinda worried and thought maybe we were in some danger. Eddie just sat there in his bunk and said not to worry, it was just practice. I tell you the truth, I don't know why they would shoot a fellow like that. I don't think it was right.

—— No, he never talked about deserting. He griped about being drafted, but so did a lot of guys. He was just married, and he didn't want to go to the army. Like I told you, when he was cleaning his gun that time, he said he would never shoot it. He told me he didn't even like to shoot at animals . . . never went hunting or anything like that. I never saw him sore at anybody. He was awful serious, and never made jokes or anything. I remember he looked real sincere and straight at you when he talked.

—— We debarked at Edinburgh, and I remember Eddie handed four or five letters to a Scotch Red Cross girl and asked her to mail them to his wife. That way they wouldn't go through censorship. We went by train to Plymouth, England, where we practiced a little hedgerow fighting — something new for us. Eddie did some practice shooting, and he wasn't a bad shot. Then they sent us to Omaha Beach.

[125]

A sample of Eddie's impressions of England:

Aug. 16. Well, darling, after being in England for the past couple of days it seems to be a nice place. The people over here are pretty friendly. In fact I kind of like them. It sure is odd to hear them talk. I'm sure if you was here you'd like it yourself. Some day when this is over with you and I and the baby will come here for a visit. It's really beautiful. You think it's nice in Michigan. Well you should be here. All the homes are just about made alike. I can't describe it on paper.

In France the Slovik-Tankey-Thompson group spent five nights in the vicinity of Omaha Beach, while their papers were processed through the Third Replacement Depot at Mortain. Here are excerpts from two of Slovik's letters:

Aug. 20. Darling there isn't much I can tell you yet about France. The place I'm in is all torn up. The wine is all gone. The only thing there is for us to drink is cider. I don't like the cider at all. It tastes like you know what.

Aug. 22. Right now dear I have my tent up and I'm sleeping outside on the ground. I'm sitting on my helmet and writing you this letter on my knees. You can see for yourself how much I miss all the comforts of home. The place I'm in looks pretty bad. I don't know how the French people can stand it. Some of them are nice and friendly and some of them are pretty mean. In a way I don't blame them. They went thru a lot of trouble. Darling I pray that nothing happens to me so that I can come back to you where I belong.

—— On August 25th, Tankey recalls, we left Omaha Beach early in the morning, walking. Some place about five miles from the beach we were issued ammunition by a noncom and told that we had been assigned to G Company, 109th Infantry. Then twelve of us got into a truck with this noncom . . . me and Eddie and, yeah, I remember Thompson: I didn't know Thompson well. We drove toward Elbeuf for four or five hours, and saw a lot of destruction and dead bodies. At first it got us, but after a while we got sort of used to it. Eddie noticed it and acted about like the rest of us.

Veterans of the Normandy fighting concede that Slovik could hardly have received a more shocking introduction to war than the drive to Elbeuf, which is a small city on the south bank of the Seine about eighty miles northwest of Paris. As the German Seventh Army was compressed into the "Falaise Pocket," the fleeing German columns were forced into the open roads in daylight, and they were massacred by rocket-firing planes. The Germans, being short of gasoline, still used horse-drawn artillery; so what Slovik and the eleven other dogfaces in that truck saw was mile after mile of charred, gutted, mangled wreckage: men, horses, guns, wagons, trucks, tanks . . . a charred body, ghostly, looking almost alive, still sitting at the burned-off steering wheel of a charred truck.

In Elbeuf that afternoon SS troops were fighting, trying to hold open a river-crossing for remnants of their Seventh Army, while artillerymen of the 28th Division were shooting up these German efforts to cross the river.

—— As we got close to Elbeuf, Tankey recalls, we heard a lot of firing. We detrucked out at the edge of the city, and, as it got dark, we began making our way into town, looking for our outfit. A lot of shells were going over, and we were fired on two or three times. We didn't have an officer, just this one noncom. Close to midnight we got to this open lot and the noncom said dig in. We did. I dug a good deep hole and so did Eddie. A lot of shells were going over. We dug in good and deep. As for Eddie, I guess he was scared — I sure as hell was — he was just human. Like I say, we dug these holes and we would yell back and forth to each other. There was a lot of heavy shelling. Then after a while it let up, it got quiet. Then some tanks came in. We thought it was the krauts. But Eddie yelled: "Thank God, it's Canadians." We didn't know where our outfit was and couldn't find out. The Canadians said we might as well join up with them. We did. We wrote a letter to our regiment and told them we had lost them. Eddie knew I was sending the letter and told me to spell his name right. He never thought of it as deserting. He never talked to me about deserting, but he talked a lot about going home. Eddie and I were the only two that went with the Canadians, and even him and me got split up, but I saw him on a truck going through town the next day. I hollered at him, and we got together again.

That is Tankey's 1953 recollection of the events of the night of August 25, 1944, which, the United States later was to charge, constituted Slovik's "first desertion." And here are Tankey's recollections of the same night as of January 8, 1945 — contained in a letter he wrote to his wife from a hospital in England:

Twelve of us were assigned to the 109th Infantry, and went on a truck to the town of Elbeuf, France. We were told to get off and walk into the town and meet up with our outfit. We got off and started walking. When we walked a mile or so we had shots fired at us, we all ducked for cover, and shells started to drop around us. What a experience for a rookie. We were all separate and it was dark and more shells started to come and I really started digging like I never dug before. Shells started to drop near me, what a feeling, and I was really scared. Yes, I prayed, too, and it lifted the shelling, and I thanked God. Then the moon came out and I was laying flat on the ground in my hole, looking at the heavens with clouds around. Then near morning I heard tanks and I thought it was the jerries, but thank god it was the Canadians. So our outfit moved so fast we couldn't catch up.

Since Tankey was wounded on November 5th and Slovik was court-martialed on November 11th, Tankey was not available to testify in Slovik's defense. However, since Slovik himself chose to stand mute, and his defense offered no objection to the admission of his hand-printed "confession," there is little reason to believe Tankey would have been called.

Private Thompson, sole witness for the United States as to this First Desertion, could not be located in 1953.

Here is a portion of his testimony as analyzed in one of the legal reviews:

After moving along the edge of the city they reached an open lot where they "dug in" at about 2300 hours. Thompson saw accused with the group at this time. Between 2300 and 2330 hours the replacements, including accused, entered the city of Elbeuf to join Company G. There were "a lot of troop movements and shelling" and

"it took quite a while because there was a lot of confusion. We moved around some but stayed close together so none of us would get lost."

Thompson knew accused was at Elbeuf with the group about 0100 hours 26 August because he knew and recognized accused's voice. This was the last time he "saw" him, however, and so far as he knew, accused was not present for duty with his company at any time thereafter. The company remained at Elbeuf until Canadian troops took over, then proceeded toward Paris.

Therefore, Tankey and Thompson agree that the noncom gave an order, about 11 P.M., to dig in. Everybody heard that order. But apparently — and according to

Thompson — there was a subsequent order to move out, to move deeper into the city in search of Company G. Thompson and a few others of these replacements *did* join Company G in Elbeuf. And Thompson insisted that he "heard" Slovik with the group after they had left the holes but before they joined the company.

Tankey, on the other hand, claims that the order to move out of the holes never reached his ears, and he is positive that Slovik, like himself, never left his hole until the Canadians had been identified.

Slovik's version is contained in the confession he wrote on October 9th, the morning after his Second Desertion:

[Hand-printed in ink]
I Pvt. Eddie D. Slovik #36896415 confess to the Desertion of the United States Army. At the time of my Desertion we were in Albuff in France. I come to Albuff as a Replacement. They were shelling the town and we were told to dig in for the night. The following morning they were shelling us again. I was so scared nerves and trembling that at the time the other Replacements moved out I couldn't move. I stayed their in my foxhole till it was quite and I was able to move. I then walked in town. Not seeing any of our troops so I stayed over night at a French hospital. The next morning I turned myself over to the Canadian Provost Corp. After being with them six weeks I was turned over to American M. P. They turned me lose. I told my commanding officer my story. I said that if I had to go out their again I'd run away. He said their was nothing he could do

for me so I ran away again AND I'LL RUN AWAY AGAIN
IF I HAVE TO GO OUT THEIR.

Signed   Pvt. Eddie D. Slovik

A. S. N. 36896415

What truly happened to Private Slovik as he crouched
there in his hole, in the darkness, alone, at Elbeuf, with
shells bursting over his head? Did he "freeze," as might
have been predicted? Was he so "scared, nervous and
trembling" that he actually *couldn't* move out of the
hole? Or did he stay in the hole by premeditated plan?
He kept his word: he never fired his rifle.

Whatever happened, Eddie Slovik had decided that
once under fire was enough for him.

3

This Canadian outfit that Tankey and Slovik allied
themselves with — the 13th Provost Corps — was made
up of eighteen soldiers headed by a sergeant major. The
unit was equipped with six motorcycles, four jeeps, a
cook truck, and a heavy-duty repair and tow truck. A
roving, highly mobile outfit. Apparently they followed
the combat troops and posted notices in towns, in various languages, instructing the citizenry in the provisions
of martial law. Since Slovik and Tankey were both
"damn good guys," handy on KP, resourceful foragers,
do anything in the world for you, these Canadians
simply appropriated them in the spirit of lend-lease
and put them to work. They gave them a German "blitz

[132   ]

buggy" for transportation, and Tankey even received mail by having his wife address her letters to a Lance Corporal Gordon.

—— Those Canadians were sure good to us, Tankey recalls. They treated us good, and we had enough to eat, but it was bully beef all the time. Bully beef for breakfast, dinner and supper. One day I said to Eddie: "Did your mother ever make potato pancakes?" Every Polack eats potato pancakes. "Sure," he said. So we tried to remember between us how you make potato pancakes. We went out and stole some potatoes. The Frenchman yelled at us but we got potatoes. We knew how to ask for eggs. "Ouefs" — that's what the French call them. We traded for some of these "ouefs" and we tried to figure out how to grate the potatoes. We tried to make the French understand "potato grater." They brought us all kinds of things, but no grater. Finally Eddie figured something out. They had these cans for coffee and stuff. Eddie took the lid from one of them and punched holes in it with a hammer and nails. Then we used that for a potato grater. We had to grate an awful lot of potatoes. Our hands were all cut up and bloody. But, boy, those Canadians sure went for those pancakes. They kept after us all the time for more potato pancakes: we sure started something.

—— With the Canadians we went back toward the seashore . . . Calais and Bologne. In some little town near Calais Eddie and I heard about a warehouse that the

Germans had held. We went to it and found a big piece of meat, about an eighty-pound shank, frozen solid. We cut it up and fried it in about twenty-five pounds of margarine we got from the warehouse. It sure tasted good, and those Canadians appreciated it. We ate some good meals off that shank.

—— Whatever town we went to, the Canadians would requisition the best houses and stay in them. They taught Eddie and I to drive their motorbikes. We traveled a lot at night — you got so you could see in the dark. The Canadians had this German blitz buggy — like a jeep, only bigger and has five speeds. Eddie and I painted it up — Eddie was a good painter — and put U.S. and Canada on it to disguise it. Later on the higher-ups made us get rid of it for fear it would be spotted by the Germans. Eddie and I sold it to a Frenchman. We even gave him a receipt.

—— While we were with the Canadians Eddie gave up carrying any ammunition. He carried stationery in his cartridge belt all the time instead. He would have it all folded up small. He collected it from the Red Cross everywhere we went, and he continually wrote letters to his wife. He never carried ammunition from that time on. But he didn't seem any different than he had ever been. I bunked with him, and I sure never thought of him as yellow . . . no, I did not. He was a real serious kind of guy, and he was good to me. He did me lots of favors. One time in particular. I got a flesh wound, and he took me in a jeep into this little French town and found a civilian doctor for me. But he did favors for everybody. . . . Those Canadians sure liked him. . . . They'll sure be surprised to learn that Eddie Slovik was shot as a coward. It's not right to shoot a man like that.

—— Eddie just didn't hate anybody, not even the Germans. When we were on our way back to Spa, Belgium, we saw a lot of villagers, very excited. They had a German pilot. They had torn his clothes and beat him up some. Eddie and me took the German into custody and he went with us in the jeep. Eddie treated him nice and friendly and gave him cigarets. We got to Spa — that's a health-resort town and they had a headquarters there. We got there in the evening about eight. We reported we had this prisoner, picked up from the Belgians. The sergeant said we were responsible for the prisoner and should keep him with us all night. We asked for a room on the seventh floor: we figured he wouldn't want to get away bad enough to jump that far. Eddie kept on giving him cigarets all evening. I wouldn't have done that for a kraut. Anyhow, we were going to take turns watching the prisoner that night. It ended up we both went to sleep, and who do you think wakes us up in the morning — the kraut. He went to breakfast with us, had the same as we did. Eddie gave him more cigarets. A lot of guys were noticing how friendly Eddie was treating this kraut — and they didn't like it. But

Eddie didn't mean any harm: he just wasn't mad at anybody.

—— Eddie never drank to amount to anything. And whenever he met girls he talked about his wife. One time in Ghent we were in a pub and drinking some. A guy told us there were two girls outside from Detroit. I finally went out and talked to them. One spoke English but with quite an accent. She said: "I hear there are two Yankees in this place so I came to see. I used to work in Detroit in a tobacco factory at Junction and Fort." She lived about four or five blocks down the way. She took me and Eddie to her house and introduced us to her grandfather. He used to live in Kansas City. He brought out some wine. Eddie began to smile a little, with the wine and good company. He brought out the pictures of his wife and showed them around. He told everybody about her. This girl we were with was named Suzanne. She said we might as well stay all night. But Eddie wouldn't stay. He went away, and next morning he was around early to see if I was all right. The people there said they would like to have some gas to go to a funeral. Eddie was gone like a flash and he came back with two five-gallon cans of gas. They wanted to pay us for it, but we wouldn't take any money.

—— Now how can you shoot a guy like that? I still can't believe it! He'd do anything in the world for you! Best-hearted guy I ever met. Everybody liked him. But he was serious — never drank or laughed much. We used to go to the pubs at night, and it never cost us any-thing because we were the only Yanks around, and everything was on the house. They would play "The Stars and Strips Forever" whenever we went in.

—— Me and Eddie were with the Canadians about forty-five days. We had sent this letter to the 109th tell-ing them we had got lost, and radiograms were sent out. Eddie was in favor of rejoining the 109th. He never talked to me about deserting. He talked about going home all the time. He felt like he had never got a break in his life till he got married — then the army took him. He didn't like it. A lot of guys, plenty of them, felt the same way. But I don't believe he intended to desert. If he had, then why did he go with me back to the 109th? There were plenty of ways he could have kept from going back.

By failing to catch up with the 109th on August 26th, Tankey and Slovik had missed the big parade on the 29th: the whole division marching through Paris. They had also missed the big fight at the Siegfried Line — dragons' teeth, the blasting of the West Wall by hard-slugging rifle companies . . . like Company G. They had missed an inspiring event: the crossing of the Our River, during which Sergeant Francis J. Clark, K Company, 109th, repeatedly rallied reluctant men, killed many Germans, won, from the United States, the Congres-sional Medal of Honor.

Slovik had done a good job with the Canadians: cooking potato pancakes, helping people attend funerals, dispensing cigarets to weary German pilots. No doubt about it: Eddie Slovik was a damn goodhearted guy, do anything in the world for you. Anything, that is, except the *duty* to which he had been assigned.

Unfortunately, Slovik had not been assigned to the Red Cross. Brotherhood was not his business. He had been trained and sent to Europe for the primary purpose of killing Germans, and on October 8th what G Company, 109th Regiment, needed was killers. For on that date the company, the regiment, and the division were reorganizing, integrating replacements, preparing to jump into the "Green Hell of Hürtgen."

The United States — and Dutch Cota and Jim Rudder — expected every man, including Private Slovik, to do his duty.

4

When Tankey and Slovik reported to 28th Division headquarters at Elsenborn, Belgium, on October 5th, they were not under arrest. No charges had been placed against them. They had been carried as missing or absent without leave on the company rolls; their cases were not extraordinary. During the rush across France following the Falaise action, many soldiers had been separated from their units, some of them with good reason, some of them just for lack of initiative in keeping up. Some of these absences were attributable to the replacement system used, for the first time by the United States, in the Second War ... the system demonstrated in the Slovik case ... the system under which a corporal takes a dozen rookie privates and tries to deliver them under fire to a company fighting "in or near Elbeuf."

The protests against this replacement system were expressed in the bitter cry, heard everywhere: "Don't send us any more replacements; we haven't got time to bury them."

Tankey and Slovik reached 109th regimental headquarters near Rocherath, Belgium, on October 7th; and here is Tankey's account of his subsequent experience:

—— I explained how we got lost from our outfit. Then they sent me and Eddie to Company G. It was a good outfit. I got a little mad at one of the officers. That was the only thing I ever had against the army. This officer kept the cablegram about my father's death, and I never did find out about it until my wife wrote me. I was pretty mad and I had a fight with the guy. He was going to take some kind of action about it, but we both got wounded. I was next to him then in the hospital. I got to know him pretty well. He told me he was sorry about the cablegram: that he forgot to give it to me.

—— My squad was caught in a barrage and I was hit with shrapnel in Hürtgen on November 5th. We had killed or wounded about forty-five Germans. Everything was quiet, and then a couple of German medics came out to look at the wounded. They got away and probably told our position. We were under a very heavy barrage. The guy next to me got it really bad. It was a day or two before I got to a hospital, and they kept me in hospitals until March 13th.

So all that the United States expected of Tankey and Slovik, even as late as October 8th, was that they get up on the line and do some "closing with the enemy" — so that everybody could go home. This Tankey did, and he was lucky: when he got shot he got it in the leg.

Tankey insists he thought Slovik, too, would try to soldier, despite his statement that he would never shoot his rifle and his having substituted stationery for shells in his ammunition belt. But when Eddie reported to Captain Ralph O. Grotte, commander of Company G, in a farmhouse near Rocherath, on the afternoon of October 8th, he told the captain that he was "too scared, too nervous" to serve with a rifle company, and that unless he could be kept in a rear area he'd run away. The captain shook his head, said there was nothing he could do, and assigned Eddie to the 4th Platoon. Here is the result as analyzed in a legal review of the court-martial proceedings:

Accused [Slovik] was never present with the company for duty except on 8 October for one or two hours. On that day a battalion sergeant major brought him to the company command post where Captain Grotte assigned him to the

4th Platoon, turned him over to the platoon leader and forbade him to leave the company area unless he had permission from the company commander. The platoon leader conducted accused to his platoon and introduced him to his squad leader. Thereafter accused came to Captain Grotte and inquired of him if he could be tried for being absent without leave. Grotte told him he would find out and caused him to be placed in arrest and returned to his platoon area, where Grotte directed him to stay. About an hour later Slovik returned to Grotte and asked him, "If I leave now will it be desertion?" Grotte replied that it would be. Slovik left and thereafter he was not seen in the company area, nor was he present for duty.

This account is based on the testimony of Captain Grotte at the court-martial. The captain, Serial Number 01290237, whose home address in 1944 was listed in army records as Northwood, North Dakota, could not be located for this investigation in 1953.

Tankey's recollections are as follows:

—— We reported to the officer in charge. I don't know his name. I talked to him first, came out of his office, then Eddie went in. After a while Eddie came out, without his gun, walking fast. The officer came out and said to me: "Soldier, you better stop your buddy. He is getting himself into serious trouble." Eddie walked right past me without looking at me. He started walking down a little hill, fast. I ran after him, fifty or a hundred yards, caught up with him, grabbed him by the shoulder, and stopped him.

——— "Come on back, Eddie," I said. "You don't want to do this."

——— He just looked at me, dead serious. "Johnny," he said, "I know what I'm doing." He jerked away and kept going. I figured he would be back. I never saw him again. When he didn't come back, I figured he had been assigned to some other outfit. I never knew he was in trouble.

It can't be ascertained where Slovik spent the night of October 8th — probably in a Belgian barn — but about 8:30 A.M. next day, October 9th, he came to the Military Government Detachment, 112th Infantry, in Rocherath, and handed a cook a green slip of paper containing handwriting, and told the cook that he had made a confession. The cook informed Lieutenant Thomas F. Griffin, and Griffin telephoned the 109th Infantry to send someone for him. An MP came and returned Slovik to the orderly room of the 109th, and handed the slip of paper to Lieutenant Wayne L. Hurd, the MP officer. Hurd delivered the slip to Lieutenant Colonel Ross C. Henbest.

The green slip of paper, a U.S. Army Post Exchange flower-order form, with writing in ink on both sides, was Slovik's confession — already reported here in full. And in it Eddie said of his talk with Captain Grotte:

I told my commanding officer my story. I said that if I had to go out their again I'd run away. He said their was nothing he could do for me so I ran away again and I'll run away again if I have to go out their.

(In almost every case in his letters where Slovik uses the word *there* or *their* he employs the spelling *their*.)

Colonel Henbest, former instructor at Gulf Coast Military Academy, Gulfport, Mississippi, warned Eddie that the written confession could be damaging to him, and suggested that he take it back and destroy it. When Eddie refused, Colonel Henbest then entered this record on the reverse side of the slip:

This statement is made in the presence of Lt. Col. Ross C. Henbest 0237158 and 1st Lt. Wayne Hurd 0463853.

I have been told that this statement can be held against me and that I made it of my own free will and that I do not have to make it.

Signed: Eddie D. Slovik

Above statement was signed in the presence of the undersigned:

Signed: Ross C. Henbest
Lt. Col., Infantry
Signed: Wayne L. Hurd
1st Lt., Infantry

Slovik was then confined in the division stockade, awaiting action against him by the United States.

5

Why had Slovik acted so deliberately, so recklessly? Company G was not under fire on the afternoon of October 8th. Why didn't Slovik go ahead and pretend to soldier, then "get lost" again when the regiment moved into action? Why had he returned to the company only to tell his commander that he couldn't or wouldn't perform the duties of a rifleman? Why did he "confess" — without being asked — that he had stayed in the hole at Elbeuf because he was scared? Why didn't he claim that he had stayed in the hole because he failed to hear the order? This claim was so common that it was standard operating procedure. Above all, why did Slovik put all this *in writing* in violation of all the rules of self-preservation in any army?

The unanimous conclusion among the legal reviewers was this:

This evidence leads inevitably to the conclusion that accused deliberately absented himself on 8 October with the intent of deserting the military service so that he would be tried by court-martial and incarcerated and thus avoid the hazardous duty and shirk the important service of action against the enemy.

Many American soldiers took this course; many of them *sought* court-martial and incarceration; and by the lawyers who reviewed the case for the United States, Slovik was credited with calculation: he called his commander's attention to his desertion . . . he wrote out his confession, in which he may even have misrepresented his own actions at Elbeuf . . . he stated in writing that

[144]

he would continue to run away — all this as part of a calculated effort to *make certain* that he would be jailed, to *make certain* that he would never risk the possibility of going under fire again, to *make certain* his safe return to his wife and his apartment and his privacy.

But is it possible that Slovik was only telling the truth? That he was, truly, so "scared, nervous and trembling" at Elbeuf that he couldn't move out of his hole? Was he only being forthright when he told his commander that he *couldn't* serve with a rifle company?

Jail, to Eddie Slovik, was a place of refuge — the womb to which he thought he could always return if life became too tough, too demanding, on the outside. Remember what he said the night the priest told him he couldn't be married at St. Barbara's? "Maybe I ought to go back to jail and forget about it all." Remember how, after the draft notice had stunned him, he purposely failed to report to his parole officer in the half hope that he'd be arrested and returned to Ionia?

Returning to jail, as a protective tactic, had been in the back of Eddie's mind since the night he received the draft notice. Just when and how to effect this return ... He, no doubt, was thinking about this during some of those periods when Tankey noticed his seriousness and preoccupation. Perhaps Eddie finally made up his mind there in the hole at Elbeuf: whenever the possibility of his going under fire approached again, he'd make certain his return to his haven: he'd do what, to him, he should have done when he got the draft notice.

But why did he risk the written confession? This green flower-order form with his handwriting on it is the first clue to the mystery of why Slovik was the *one* deserter who was shot. Why did he take this seemingly unnecessary risk, then persist in it after being warned by Colonel Henbest?

The answer is another question: what risk? Why should Private Slovik have thought that, even with his written confession, he was risking anything more than the jail he sought? Not in "modern times" — not since 1864 — had an American deserter risked more than confinement in a safe, comparatively comfortable jail, with the probability of being released a few months after the war was over.

Eight . . .

T HE approximately one hundred days from the time Private Slovik was confined to the 109th Regimental Prisoner of War Enclosure, October 9, 1944, until his execution, January 31, 1945, was one of the most difficult periods in the history of the United States Army and of the 28th Division. It was a period of hard luck . . . of galling disappointment . . . of having to crush, at great cost, senseless, illogical resistance . . . of being told that the war was over, then having to watch your friends thrown into mattress covers and buried in frozen ground . . . of celebrating victory, then having to die with your feet wet.

All this was due to the senselessness of the modern totalitarian state — and to a well-intentioned American leadership with a shortage of wisdom. After the breakthrough in Normandy — the gallant, spirited race across France — the war, it was said, was "over." Germany was beaten; the armistice or surrender was a matter of hours, days at the most. Were not the Germans realists?

Hadn't they quit on French soil in 1918? Would an old, professional soldier like Gerd von Rundstedt continue a "senseless" war? Even Napoleon's devoted marshals, tearfully but firmly, were capable of throwing down the Little Corporal in 1814 as the price of peace with Britain. Hitler was "kaput."

Remember how Slovik's Ouija board had told him, when he was on furlough in July, that the war in Europe would end in September, 1944? Remember how he wrote his wife from Fort Meade that he had read in his papers a confirmation of this prediction? In one of Tankey's letters he tells of how, lying there in the hole at Elbeuf, he saw a sign in the heavens which he interpreted to mean that the war would end on October 5th.

The Americans who paraded through Paris on August 29th felt, almost to a man, that they were home free. If they had dodged all the lead in Normandy, they were going home alive — without even a Purple Heart. The war was "over" — the papers were full of it.

But it wasn't over; it had only begun. Hitler had everything to gain and nothing to lose by continuing the war right down until rifle butts were beating on his bunker door. His marshals yearned to throw him down, but he survived the effort to kill him . . . and old Marshal von Rundstedt, from his knees, was capable of the Ardennes counteroffensive.

The result was a Valley Forge with action for America's citizen-soldiers. Here is an excerpt from the 28th Division's history:

The fighting in Hürtgen Forest [it began November 2nd] was the most difficult ever faced by the Keystone outfit. Weather and terrain did not favor the division. The concentrated German artillery had a terrifying effect. Casualties were heavy, withdrawals were necessary.

Casualty figures for the Hürtgen fighting list a total loss of 248 officers and 5452 enlisted men. Personnel changes were so rapid that units could not recover to a high degree of combat effectiveness. Reinforcements were rushed into the line with so much speed and in such large numbers that proper organizing of units was impossible. On November 8th, for example, 515 replacements were integrated into the 2nd Battalion, 112th Infantry alone.

For the difficult terrain, 47 cargo carriers, commonly called "weasels," were furnished the division. Of these 47 tracked vehicles, 22 were lost in action.

The problem of the medical personnel was particularly difficult. Long litter hauls were imperative. In one sector it was necessary to hand-carry the wounded almost four miles through the tangles of a pine forest shattered by artillery fire. Two battalion aid stations were cut off for a three-day period. Collecting stations were subjected to enemy shell fire. Casualties in the Schmidt-Kommerscheidt area were so heavy it was necessary to effect a four-hour truce for removal of the wounded.

It was during this winter of wet snow, fierce casualties, cold rations, prodigal use of replacements, and "senseless," static warfare that the desertion rate boomed. A commander could go up at night expecting to find two hundred men on the line and be lucky to find seventy. There was an epidemic of "combat fatigue," and division commanders swore at psychiatrists.

There were thousands of men seeking courts-martial — and confinement — as a tactic to evade combat, and Eddie Slovik was one of them. On October 23rd he addressed this letter to Antoinette:

Mommy, I guess you are wondering how come I am writing my mail on red cross paper. Well, darling I'm in a little trouble and I've been working for the red cross for the past two weeks and that's where I'm getting my paper. Please don't worry about me cause I'm alright. I'm only worried about what they are going to do to me. . . . Please, mommy, I beg you to wait for me. I'll let you know just as soon as I know how much time I get. If it's too much then I'll ask you to get a divorce. I won't have you waiting three or four years for me. . . . It seems to me, my darling, that I have always been in trouble. Everything happens to me. I've never had a streak of luck in my life. The only luck I had in my life was when I married you. I knew it wouldn't last because I was too happy. I knew they wouldn't let me be happy. I only pray to the Lord to help me and you my love.

That's the last of his letters to Antoinette: *I knew they wouldn't let me be happy.*

On October 26th Slovik was transferred to the division stockade at Rott, Germany, where he was confined

[150   ]

until after his court-martial. One of the men in charge of this enclosure was Sergeant Edward Needles, a heavy, dark-haired, one-time National Guarder, who now runs a luncheonette with his brother at 734 S. 5th Street, Philadelphia.

—— Sure, I remember Slovik, Needles recalls. He was just one of the kids bucking for a court-martial so he could stay out of the line. We had our share of them. A goodhearted kid. Do anything I told him to. Sweep up, handle garbage, load supplies. . . . He was a damn good worker . . . never complained. Nice-looking kid, too. We had him around two or three weeks.

—— I remember one day in particular. A couple of other kids who had taken off were having their court-martials, and Slovik was waiting for them to come back. The stockade was in a barn, and there was a sort of hay-loft and Slovik was sitting up there with his feet hanging down and chewing on a stalk of hay. These other kids came back and they were happy as hell.

—— "How much didja get?" Slovik hollered at 'em.

—— "Twenty years," they hollered back, and they seemed happy.

—— "I'll settle for twenty years right now," Slovik said. "How long you think you'll have to stay in after the war's over?"

—— "Aw, maybe six months," one of the kids said.

—— That's how it was. I remember the day Slovik came back after his court. They had thrown the book at

[151   ]

him . . . death. He wasn't so happy. He and the kids around figured he might be stuck in jail for two or three years after the war was over. Of course it never occurred to him or any other prisoner — even after he got the sentence — that he would actually be shot.

2

In the 28th Division the ranking legal representative of the United States was the former district attorney of Selinsgrove, Pennsylvania, Lieutenant Colonel Henry J. Sommer — division judge advocate. He was born at Hollidaysburg, Pennsylvania; educated at Dickinson College, Carlisle, Pennsylvania. A tall, blond, quiet man, Colonel Sommer elected to stay in the army's "JAG Corps" after the war; and in 1953 he was living with his wife and two teenage children at Fort Bragg, North Carolina, where he was post judge advocate.

In his position Colonel Sommer had two responsibilities. First, to the United States. It was his duty to try to see that military law was enforced in a manner which would contribute to discipline in the 28th Division . . . in a manner which would deter military offense . . . in a manner which would help the division to destroy the enemy. His second responsibility was to the individual soldier — to try to safeguard all the rights which this nation extends to a citizen-soldier even under the extremities of combat.

In the Slovik case Colonel Sommer proceeded as he

had in similar cases. Slovik was a criminal. . . . He had committed a crime against the United States . . . a crime which was a threat to the effectiveness of the military organization. Moreover, a human being, an individual soldier, was in trouble: he had assumed a position of defiance for which the law said he should be shot.

—— Of course I remember Slovik, Colonel Sommer recalls. I remember him well. I saw him on three occasions.

—— Since his case was such an unusual one and since he had never even tried soldiering in a rifle company, I had him brought up to my office. That was probably about October 29th. It was late afternoon. Two MPs had him in a jeep; he was sitting in the back seat, handcuffed. I walked out on the road to talk to him. He was a nice-looking fellow; not insolent, but calculating.

—— "Slovik," I said, "you're in trouble and I'd like to help you get out of it. We don't like to court-martial anybody; we do that only as a final resort. If you will go back to your outfit and soldier I'll ask the general if he will suspend action on your court-martial. I'll even try to get you a transfer to another regiment where nobody will know what you have done and you can make a clean start."

—— He shook his head. "I'm not going back up there in the line," he said. "I can't serve in a rifle company."

—— "Why don't you try?" I said. "You haven't even

[153   ]

been with your outfit long enough to know what it's like."

—— "No," he replied. "I'd be willing to take a job way back from the line with a quartermaster outfit or something like that, but if I can't get that, then give me my court-martial."

—— "Well, we can't transfer everybody out of a rifle company to a warehouse or a supply dump just because they would prefer that sort of soldiering," I told him. "You realize you'll get at least a DD and a heavy sentence to confinement if you go to trial. You might even get a death sentence. Desertion in time of war is a capital offense. You're making a big mistake if you don't go back up there and try it."

—— "No, I've made up my mind," he said. "I'll take my court-martial."

—— So I replied: "Okay, take him back to the stockade." I wasn't particularly surprised at his attitude. I had heard too many like him say, "I want my general court-martial."

Two other officers talked with Slovik before his trial: Captain Edward P. Woods, his court-appointed defense counsel, and Captain Arthur L. Burks, the division neuropsychiatrist.

Mr. Woods, who is not a lawyer, is now in business in Philadelphia. . . . He is the father of four children. That the *one* deserter who was executed had the benefit of his

[154   ]

counsel — this is something less than a source of pride to Mr. Woods. Often assigned as defense counsel in courts-martial, he had shown his ability on numerous occasions; many of the defendants represented by Mr. Woods had been found not guilty.

—— There just wasn't much I could do, he says. Slovik had made his mind up.

Nevertheless, to carry out his assigned duty, Mr. Woods, after interviewing Slovik, obtained all the facts in connection with the charge and carefully advised Slovik as to his legal rights. He determined that there were no witnesses on Slovik's behalf and learned that the psychiatric examination precluded any defense on the grounds of mental disorder. Slovik pleaded Not Guilty, stood mute, and waited for the judgment of the court.

—— I liked Slovik. There was something about him that made him different from any other man I had tried to help. He didn't strike me as being a coward. I don't know what it was.

The record of the Slovik trial has been carefully reviewed by several fine lawyers, and there is no criticism of the manner in which Mr. Woods carried out his assignment and tried to safeguard Slovik's interests.

Dr. Burks, who was division psychiatrist during most of the combat period, has nothing to add to his formal report. He examined — interviewed is his word —

Slovik on October 26th, and his report is part of the official file, though it was not introduced as evidence:

I have this date interviewed Pvt. Eddie D. Slovik, Company G, 109th Infantry, and find him to show no evidence of mental disease at this time, and I consider him sane and responsible for his actions at this time. There is no evidence that he was other than sane and responsible at the time of his alleged offenses. He has never sought medical attention regarding any physical or nervous complaints by his own admission.

Signed: Arthur L. Burks
Division Neuropsychiatrist

3

In the 28th Division Colonel Sommer represented Law, and Dr. Burks represented Medicine, mental variety. Both of these officers examined Eddie Slovik to see if they should recommend to command authority that Slovik be given a concession by the United States . . . the concession of the safe duty he demanded. Colonel Sommer decided against any such recommendation, and Dr. Burks confined himself to the simple report of no evidence of mental disease. Because his field is the more controversial, the action of Dr. Burks will be more widely debated.

What about psychiatry in the Slovik case? If Slovik had received more elaborate psychiatric examination, would the United States have been well advised to have made a concession to him? Either the concession of not being inducted into the army at all, or the concession of safe duty, or, at least, the concession of his life? Did the United States *owe* Slovik such elaborate examination? And should Generals Eisenhower and Cota have required such examination before sending Slovik to his death?

These questions can only be answered by each individual who considers the case. All that can be done here is to offer brief clues as to the attitude toward psychiatry on the part of those who held command authority in the 28th Division and in the ETO: Cota and Eisenhower.

The conflict in the Second War between the "West Point mind" and the psychiatrists was enormously intriguing. The West Pointers — the men of authority — insisted on simplicity. In big wars men with authority naturally yearn for simple rules like: *an able-bodied man who won't fight for his country doesn't deserve to live.* The psychiatrists — the men who could only advise and who did not have responsibility — challenged these simple rules. The West Pointers cherished individual responsibility; the psychiatrists cast doubts on it. The psychiatrists were handicapped in this conflict by being in disagreement among themselves; and, moreover, they lacked detection devices. There are devices for detecting physical illness — thermometer, stethoscope, X ray

— but there are no such devices for detecting and proving mental disorder.

Here is a 1953 sample of General Cota's disciplined, West Point mind:

—— I never was impressed with what they called our "orientation program" during the war. I think it is more effective to teach men traditions and obligations. Whenever I spoke to men under my command I put it as simply as I could: "Men, for every *right* that you enjoy there is a *duty* that you must assume. You've heard a lot of talk about *rights;* now you'll hear a lot about *duty.*"

—— I didn't pay much attention to psychiatry at first, but I began giving it some thought there in England, when I heard them referring to combat fatigue as a "disease." I couldn't understand what they meant. Fatigue is an enemy that every army commander has to consider. But I thought it was peculiar and unwise to talk about fatigue as a "disease."

—— After we had landed in Normandy with the 29th Division — I was assistant division commander — we set up one of those treatment centers for combat fatigue in the rear echelon: it was not on the tables of organization. And we began noticing that a large group of our men were going back there for treatment. The division commander asked me to go back and see what was going on. So I went back.

—— I didn't interfere with anything; I just sat there and listened to a doctor interviewing these men.

—— "Have you had enough?" he'd ask them.

—— "Yeah, Doc, I've had all I want," they'd reply.

—— "Do you want to go back up to the line?"

—— "No, Doc, I've had enough."

—— I just sat there and listened to that nonsense. "What is that doctor trying to do?" I asked myself. "What does he think he can accomplish by asking men if they've had enough? These men are tired, sure. They need rest. But then they need to go back to the line. They aren't suffering from any *disease;* nothing's wrong with most of them that a few hours' rest won't cure."

—— I didn't get a good impression of psychiatry, and I so reported to the commanding officer.

—— When I took over the 28th I had one of these treatment centers set up — I've got nothing against treating exhausted men; I wanted that; and I wanted the psychiatrists to help if they could. Then one night I went back to inspect it. . . . We were at the Siegfried Line . . . and it was raining hard.

—— Well, it was a disgraceful scene, with no semblance of organization, discipline or care being shown for the soldiers. It was a place no soldier should have been, especially one suffering from combat fatigue. I was burned up! . . . And I told the division surgeon, Dr. Weest, to get us another psychiatrist.

[159   ]

—— Dr. Weest put Dr. Burks in charge, and I thought Dr. Burks did a good job for us.

Dr. Harry W. Weest is now head of the Pennsylvania Tuberculosis Sanatorium at Cresson, Pennsylvania. Here is a portion of his comment on October 22, 1953:

—— When General Cota assumed command of the 28th, he told me of a treatment center for combat exhaustion which the 29th had organized in their rear echelon despite the fact that it was not on the tables of organization. I immediately set up such a treatment center for our division.

—— Our CE cases were sent back to this center through medical channels and were given seconal in sufficient dosage to "knock them out" for twenty-four hours. They were then given hot food and a period of orientation was begun. An infantry officer was placed in charge, and, assisted by the chaplain, a special service officer, a medical officer, and the Red Cross, he supervised a program of letter writing, reading, review of the history of the division, and short road marches. These men were then asked to return to the front, and a number of them did.

—— There were not too many CE cases and only a few Section 8 Boards while the division was moving. However, in September, when we first entered Germany, the weather was cold and wet, and our troops were pinned down along the German front, the CE cases increased, and General Cota was very much concerned. He told me that the medical officers and, particularly the psychiatrists, were sending too many men back to the division clearance stations. That, in my opinion, was the reason for General Cota's dislike for psychiatrists.

—— General Cota's anger over this situation became such that while we were at Elsenborn I arranged for the First Army psychiatrist, Lieutenant Colonel William G. Srodes, to bring over the reports on CE cases of other divisions in the First Army. And even after we showed General Cota that our record on CE cases was as good as the other divisions, he was still dissatisfied.

—— On September 17th, while the rear echelon was in the vicinity of Ulflingen, General Cota came back one night after seeing the apparently poor work being done by a psychiatrist in some adjoining area. He was highly critical of what he had observed.

—— I thought General Cota was right in criticizing that particular psychiatrist. I also thought that Dr. Burks did an excellent job. He discussed the Slovik case with me and told me of his report.

—— As for General Cota's blaming the medical branch for the number of CE cases . . . well, here's the story: in combat, when the enemy is being pushed back — when you are moving — then there are few CE cases. But when the situation becomes tough and slow and stationary and damned uncomfortable — like

Hürtgen — then the CE cases pile up, and some branch of the service must be blamed.

That was the psychiatric atmosphere in the 28th Division . . . the atmosphere surrounding the Slovik case. General Cota tolerated psychiatry; he went further — he abetted it to the extent of going outside the tables of organization. But whenever he found occasion to observe psychiatrists in action, the impression he got was not good: he relieved them, chewed them out, gave them a bad time.

4

The general court-martial in the Slovik case, which resulted in the single execution for a military offense since the Civil War, was one of the shortest such proceedings in our history. The court was convened at 10 A.M., November 11, 1944, and at 11:40 A.M. the verdict had been returned and the court adjourned.

The trial was held on the second floor of a public building in Rötgen, Germany, which is twenty miles south of Aachen, in Hürtgen Forest. On the ground floor German civilians queued up for their ration cards. Two American MPs guarded the stairs, and in a large public room on the second floor, dominated by the flag of the United States, the nine-officer court sat behind a long table. The presiding officer was Colonel Guy M. Williams, Harrisburg, Pennsylvania, division finance officer, who presided at more than a hundred general courts for the 28th.

To the left and right of Colonel Williams sat the other eight officers of the court:

Major Orland F. Leighty, Connellsville, Pennsylvania, a dentist.

Major Herbert D. White, Oklahoma City, assistant adjutant general.

Major Robert D. Montondo, Washington, D.C., a special-services officer.

Captain Benedict Kimmelman, Philadelphia, a dentist.

Captain Arthur V. Patterson, Baton Rouge, Louisiana, of the inspector general's staff.

Captain Stanley H. French, Medical Corps, Regular Army.

Captain Clarence W. Welch, Regular Army, headquarters staff.

First Lieutenant Bernard Altman, Perth Amboy, New Jersey, law member of the court. He is the only member who in 1953 was deceased. Awarded the Silver Star, the Bronze Star, and the Purple Heart, he was fatally wounded in the Bulge battle and died in German prison camp.

All of these men were staff officers, of the division staff: none of them was a combat officer. Courts generally were composed of such officers for an obvious reason: combat officers had no time for the long court sessions — on November 11th every combat officer in the 28th Division was under fire . . . the Hürtgen campaign had begun on November 2nd. And this circumstance was believed by most persons to favor the defendants: staff officers were likely to be more lenient on a Slovik than would combat officers.

The prosecutor, who sat alone, was a young practicing attorney from Antonito, Colorado, Captain John I. Green. Slovik sat at a table with his counsel, Captain Woods. The reporter was Sergeant John S. Clapper, Hollidaysburg, Pennsylvania.

Captain Green stated the general nature of the charge: violation of the 58th Article of War — desertion to avoid hazardous duty. The charges had been preferred by Captain Grotte; they had been served on Slovik on October 30th. (This was the day after he had refused the offer made to him by Colonel Sommer.)

Lieutenant Altman, as law member of the court, explained to Slovik that he had the right to challenge any member of the court for cause, and that he could exercise the right to one peremptory challenge against any member except the law member.

Captain Green asked Slovik if he objected to any member of the court. He answered no.

Slovik was then arraigned on the charge of violating the 58th Article of War, with two specifications: Elbeuf and Rocherath. He pleaded Not Guilty to each of the specifications as well as to the general charge. The first witness was Private Thompson: he told the Elbeuf story. There was virtually no cross-examination. Next was Lieutenant Hurd, the MP officer to whom Slovik had handed the green slip bearing his confession. Without objection from the defense, the confession was admitted as evidence. Then came Captain Grotte, who told of his conversations with Slovik on October 8th and of the subsequent calculated desertion. The defense had no questions for either Hurd or Grotte.

Pvt. William C. Schmidt was then called by the prosecution:

Q. What is your name, grade, and organization?
A. William C. Schmidt, Private, Military Government Detachment, 112th Infantry.
Q. Do you know this soldier who sits by his counsel here?
A. Yes sir.
Q. What is his name?
A. I don't know his name but I recognize his face.
Q. When did he come to your notice?
A. I don't remember the date but it was the second day we were in Rocherath.
Q. What were the circumstances?
A. I was detailed as a cook that day when about 8:30 this fellow came to the front door and handed me a green slip of paper with writing on it and said he had made a confession. I then asked him to come in and he came and I went on with my work. He came to the kitchen

and asked for something to eat and so I gave him some and he helped wash dishes. I told the commanding officer about him and he came to the commanding officer and gave him the green slip of paper with the confession on it.

Q. How long was he around your detachment there before this?

A. About three hours.

The last witness was Lieutenant Griffin, the officer to whom Schmidt had referred. The defense had no questions — at no point in the trial did any member of the court ask a question — and the prosecution rested. It was 10:50 A.M., and the court recessed for ten minutes.

At 11 A.M., with the court in session, Captain Woods rose and stated:

Accused understands his rights as a witness and elects to remain silent, but Defense requests that the Law Member advise the accused as to his rights as a witness.

Lieutenant Altman then rose and addressed Slovik:

Private Slovik, it is my duty to explain to you that you have the legal right to: 1) Be sworn as a witness and testify in your own behalf under oath like any other witness and be subject to cross-examination on the whole substance of any particular specification concerning which you testify in explanation or denial; 2) Make an unsworn statement either written or oral. It may be made by you or your counsel or both. It will be taken for what it appears to be worth in

[166   ]

explanation, denial, or excuse, and you will not be subject to cross-examination on it; or 3) Remain silent in which case no inference of your guilt or innocence will be drawn by the court nor will the trial judge advocate comment upon your silence in his closing argument. Take time to confer with your counsel and decide what you intend to do.

Here is the remainder of the official record:

At this point the accused conferred with his defense counsel.

Private Slovik: I will remain silent.

Defense: The defense rests.

The Prosecution made a closing argument.

The Defense made no closing argument.

Prosecution: The prosecution has nothing further to offer.

Defense: The defense has nothing further to offer.

FINDINGS
Neither the prosecution nor the defense having anything further to offer, the court was closed, and upon secret written ballot, all the members present at the time the vote was taken concurring in each finding of guilty, finds the accused:

Of Specification 1 of the Charge: "Guilty"
Of Specification 2 of the Charge: "Guilty"
Of the Charge: "Guilty"

PREVIOUS CONVICTIONS, ETC.

The court was opened, and the trial judge advocate stated, in the presence of the accused and his counsel, that he had evidence of *no* previous convictions to submit.*

The trial judge advocate then read the data as to age, pay and service as shown on the charge sheet, and verified by the accused in open court, as follows:

Age 24 8/12 yrs, Pay $60 per month. Class E Allotment to dependents, $15 per month. Class F Deduction: $22 per month. Government Insurance Deduction: $6.70 per month.

Data as to service: Inducted Bd #3, Detroit, Michigan, 3 January 44; assigned d-59 Inf Tng Bn, Cp Wolters, Tex 31 January 44; attached GFRD #1 Ft Meade Md 11 July 44; attached to GFRS 14 Aug 44; attached to 3rd Replacement Depot 19 Aug 44; assigned to Co G, 109th Inf.

Data as to restraint of accused: Confined at Regimental Prisoner of War Incl., 9 Oct 44. Confined Division Prisoner of War Inclosure 26 Oct. 44.

SENTENCE

The court was closed, and upon secret written ballot, all the members present at the time the vote was taken concurring, sentences the accused:

To be dishonorably discharged the service, to forfeit all pay and allowances due or to become due, and to be shot to death with musketry.

---

* Civilian convictions are not considered at this stage of the proceedings in a general court. At the time of this trial only offenses against the Articles of War committed during the current enlistment or obligation of the accused could be considered, and even then, in the case of an enlisted man, only those occurring during the one year next preceding the commission of any offense charged.

The court was opened, and the president announced the findings and sentence.

The court then, at 11:40 o'clock, 11 November 1944, adjourned to meet at the call of the president.

Signed: Edward P. Woods
John I. Green
Guy M. Williams

Here are Colonel Williams's recollections on the balloting:

——Well, it should be made clear that Slovik's civilian record — his having been in jail — did not and could not have influenced any member of the court. None of us knew anything about this record. All we knew was what we saw and heard: a nice-looking, healthy-looking soldier in open defiance of the authority of the United States. There was his confession: he had run away from his duties as a rifleman . . . and *he would run away again*. Given the circumstances of a division locked in bloody battle and taking heavy casualties, I didn't think I had a right to let him get away with it. That's how I felt; apparently the others felt the same way.

—— I remember I insisted on three ballots. As soon as the court was closed, we took a ballot. Unanimous: death. I then suggested that we smoke a cigaret and take a second ballot. Same result. Then just as we were about to open the court again, I said: "Well, gentlemen, this is serious. We've got to live with this the rest of our

[169   ]

lives. Let's take a third ballot." The third ballot, too, was unanimous: death.

—— That was it. I think every member of the court thought that Slovik deserved to be shot; and we were convinced that, for the good of the division, he *ought* to be shot. But in honesty — and so that people who didn't have to go to war can understand this thing — this must be said: I don't think a single member of that court actually believed that Slovik would ever be shot. I know I didn't believe it. . . . I had no reason to believe it. . . . I knew what the practice had been. I thought that the sentence would be cut down, probably not by General Cota, but certainly by Theater Command. I don't say this is what I thought *should* happen; I say it is what I felt sure *would* happen. And I thought that not long after the war ended — two or three years maybe — Slovik would be a free man.

—— When the news reached me late in January that Ike had ordered Slovik shot, I'll admit this: I probably was more surprised than Slovik was. That news hit me right between the eyes.

So when Eddie Slovik walked out of that courtroom, he had every reason to believe that his calculations had been successful. The 28th Division was mired there in Hürtgen Forest — getting the hell shot out of it — but Private Slovik was headed back to Paris . . . to safety. He was leaving the guns far behind him; he was going home to his wife, his apartment, his Pontiac. He was going to drink beer again at Nick's, see a good show at the Carmen. It might take him a little while to get there, but he had made certain his safe return.

His buddy, Tankey, had already been hit, evacuated, might be dead: Slovik had heard Thompson say this at the trial. So Slovik had been right on the afternoon of October 8th when Tankey had run down the hill after him and tried to persuade him not to take off.

Slovik was going home safe; he wasn't going to be hit; *they* weren't going to do that to him.

Nine . . .

ONCE Private Slovik had received a death sentence by general court-martial, the next move was General Cota's. Under the American system of military law, the general court is the most powerful of the courts; only a general court can impose the death sentence. The power to appoint and convene such a court is given to a division commander; and this "appointing authority" must review the decisions of the court he has created and either approve or disapprove the decisions. The "appointing authority" does not have the power to increase the severity of a sentence: he must accept the responsibility for either approval or disapproval.

In military courts the general who wields power in the name of the people of the United States cannot "wash his hands" of a Slovik case. . . . He cannot "decline to intervene," as can a governor or the President in a case involving civilians. The general must *act*; he must accept responsibility for whatever is done; and no

[172   ]

sentence is imposed until he gets his name and his seal on the document.

Therefore, Eddie Slovik was not actually under sentence of death until General Cota so declared. The general weighed this decision between November 11th and November 27th, during the Hürtgen campaign; and, for his guidance, the law required that his division judge advocate, Colonel Sommer, prepare a comprehensive review and recommendation. So Colonel Sommer was the first of the legal reviewing authorities to study the case carefully, and his review is a part of the file.

However, on November 16, 1953, in a letter to me, the Office of the Judge Advocate General took this position:

Colonel Sommer's review of the case is advisory only, and having been made pursuant to the Articles of War for the information of his commander, is a privileged communication. Accordingly, a copy thereof may not be furnished.

So Colonel Sommer's review will not be quoted directly here; and the discussion of it is based only on informal knowledge of its contents and on conversations with General Cota and Colonel Sommer.

The important point is this: in Colonel Sommer's review, for the first time in the case, Slovik's civilian record began to weigh against him. In fact, here is the second clue as to why Slovik was the *one man* who got

[173]

shot. The first clue was the confession: Slovik was the *one man* who wrote it down in black and white for *them*. The second clue is the "record": if you are going to shoot one man, it's easier to shoot one with a "record."

The Federal Bureau of Investigation furnished Colonel Sommer with the "record," and he incorporated it in his review. The "record" was there, in all its black, crisp detail, for General Cota to see. And in writing and in oral conference with General Cota, Colonel Sommer referred to this record as being one of the reasons why he did not recommend clemency.

Colonel Sommer, in conversation with me, was most forthright on this point:

"I never expected Slovik to be shot. Given the common practice up to that time, there was no reason for any of us to think that the Theater Commander would ever actually execute a deserter. But I thought that if ever they wanted a horrible example, this was one. From Slovik's record, the world wasn't going to lose much."

So you have this interesting situation: it's true that the sentence was *passed* against Slovik by men who saw him only as a determined, calculating deserter — they didn't know of the "record." But from that point on, the lawyers and generals who decided actually to shoot Slovik knew of the record, and there is no reasonable doubt that it affected the decisions.

Hence this question: Did *they* shoot Eddie Slovik

for the crime of deserting the United States Army, or did they shoot him, as he insisted, "for bread I stole when I was twelve years old"?

It was on this point that Slovik had miscalculated. There is reason to believe that he was genuinely surprised, in prison, in Paris, when he finally came to realize that his record was militating against him. He had figured it would be the other way. He had thought his record was "purty good": he had quit stealing, he had gone straight, he had learned to stay away from bad company, he had married a good woman — all this he wrote into his final plea to Eisenhower. He didn't think of his record as being "so bad," and he was stunned, embittered, to realize that the generals were dealing with him as a "con."

There is evidence that this somewhat complex bit of reasoning was not beyond him: because of his "record" the army had wanted "no part" of him when he came out of jail in 1942. Then, either despite this record or because of his good record after his release, the army had drafted him. So how could *they* now use his old record against him?

Perhaps only those of us who are in the law enforcement business, or who began our working careers as police reporters, can understand how rough such a record can be . . . how easy it is for the untrained eye to exaggerate the seriousness of a man's "*long* police record." Of course, his record is *long;* if he was arrested with a bunch of kids who had broken a lock when he was twelve years old, from that day on, whenever a chicken was stolen in his neighborhood he was arrested for investigation; and even though he was released ten minutes later, entirely innocent, a black entry went into his record. So "records" should never be judged by length alone.

This is said only because whenever I began investigating this case I found that most of the officers of the 28th Division with whom I talked had carried an eight-year misconception as to the nature of Slovik's "record." They had thought of him as having been a "hardened criminal in civil life": a felon . . . perhaps a gunman . . . some violent, authority-hating type. And they seemed to resist the truth that the most serious crime in his civilian record was the embezzlement of $59.60 worth of candy, chewing gum, cigarets and cash, taken in over the counter during a six-month period.

Eddie Slovik had a record all right; he was a criminal. But the only crime he committed in his lifetime for which the death penalty could be considered was the crime of deserting the United States Army.

It seems possible, perhaps probable, that General Cota would have approved the sentence even if there had been no civilian record. Talking with him you get the impression that he had had about enough of going up there in the dark and finding all those empty holes. And he sounds convincing when he levels down and says: "Given the situation as I knew it in November, 1944, I thought it was my duty to this country to approve that sentence. If I hadn't approved it — if I had let Slovik accomplish his purpose — then I don't know how I could have gone up to the line and looked a good soldier in the face."

General Court-Martial Order No. 27 — the order read to Slovik just before he was shot — carries this entry:

The action of the convening authority is:
HEADQUARTERS
28th Infantry Division
27 November 1944
In the foregoing case of Private Eddie D. Slovik, 36896415, Company G, 109th Infantry, only so much of the sentence as provides that the accused be shot to death with musketry is approved and the Record of Trial forwarded for action under Article of War 48.

Signed: Norman D. Cota

What is to be noted here is that General Cota modified the sentence; and the law says he can only modify a sentence in favor of the defendant. The sentence as passed by the court was:

To be dishonorably discharged the service, to forfeit all pay and allowances due or to become due, and to be shot to death with musketry.

But General Cota approved only: *to be shot to death*

with musketry. Why? What was he trying to accomplish?

The matter is still in some dispute. There was an exchange of communiqués regarding it just prior to the execution. The most likely explanation seems to be that General Cota was trying to maneuver in favor of the next of kin . . . trying to make it possible for the next of kin to receive the insurance and the accumulated pay and allowances. As evidence that this was his intention, General Cota stated to me in 1953 that he had always assumed that the next of kin received the insurance and the accumulated pay and allowances. Colonel Sommer's explanation of the change in the sentence is: the approved sentence was the one prescribed by the manual. Dishonorable discharge and forfeitures were not "the custom of the service" and were superfluous.

One last point concerning General Cota's approval. Based on their statements to me, he was the first officer connected in any way with the Slovik case who was not surprised when the theater commander confirmed the sentence *as approved*, and subsequently ordered Slovik shot.

—— No, he said, I can't honestly assert that I was surprised by the action of the theater commander. After I approved the sentence, I thought the accused would ultimately be shot. I'll admit I was surprised — maybe a little irritated — at first, when I learned that the theater commander was sending the soldier up for

[178   ]

was on parole I got myself a good job cause I was in class 4-F, the army didn't want anything to do with me at the time. So after five months out of jail I decided to get married which I did. I have a swell wife now and a good home. After being married almost a year and a half I learned to stay away from bad company which was the cause of my being in jail. Then the draft came. I didn't have to come to the army when they called me. I could of went back to jail. But I was sick of being locked up all my life so I came to the army. When I went down to the draft board, I was told that the only reason they were taking a chance on me in the army was cause I got married and had a good record after being out of jail almost two years. To my knowledge sir I have a good record in the past two years. I also have a good record as a soldier up to the time I got in this trouble. I tried my best to do what the army wanted me to do till I first ran away or should I say left the company.

I don't believe I ran away the first time as I stated in my first confession. I came over to France as a replacement, and when the enemy started to shelling us I got scared and nerves [nervous] that I couldn't move out of my fox hole. I guess I never did give myself the chance to get over my first fear of shelling. The next day their wasn't any American troops around so I turned myself over to the Canadian MPs. They in turn were trying to get in touch with my outfit about me. I guess it must have taken them six weeks to catch up with the American troops. Well sir, when I was turned over to my outfit I tried to explain to my CO just what took place, and what had happened to me. Then I asked for a transfer. Which was refused. Then I wrote my confession. I was then told that if I would go back to the line they would distroy my confession, however if I refused to go back on the line they would half to hold it against me which they did.

How can I tell you how humbley sorry I am for the sins Ive committed. I didn't realize at the time what I was doing, or what the word desertion meant. What it is like to be condemned to die. I beg of you deeply and sincerely for the sake of my dear wife and mother back home to have mercy on me. To my knowledge I have a good record since my marriage and as a soldier. I'd like to continue to be a good soldier.

Anxiously awaiting your reply, which I earnestly pray is favorable, God bless you and in your Work for victory:

I Remain Yours for Victory
Pvt. Eddie D. Slovik

This letter was never read by General Eisenhower. The general doesn't read much; he gets most of his information through the "briefing process." The letter, however, did go to the two reviewing organizations whose responsibility it was to "brief" the general on such matters.

But even if the general had been a reader, it is unlikely that he could have found time for Slovik's letter between December 12th, when it reached his office, and December 23rd, when he personally confirmed Slovik's sentence. For the German Bulge effort was launched on December 16th and was not "contained" until December 23rd.

This is the third clue as to why Eddie Slovik was the *one* deserter who got shot: timing. As he and his wife

[181   ]

said: he was the unluckiest kid in the world. Even the Germans were among *those* who balefully affected his destiny.

Here is the next entry in the court-martial order:

The action of the confirming authority is:
HEADQUARTERS
European Theater of Operations
United States Army
23 December 1944
In the foregoing case of:

Private Eddie D. Slovik, 36896415,

Company G, 109th Infantry,

the sentence, as approved, is confirmed. Pursuant to Article of War 50½, the order directing the execution of the sentence is withheld.

Signed: Dwight D. Eisenhower

Article of War 50½, which caused a month's delay in the execution of Slovik's sentence, is another safeguard for the accused in such cases. Under it not even a powerful theater commander like Eisenhower could direct the execution of such a sentence until he had been officially informed by the Office of the Judge Advocate General that "the record of trial has been examined and found legally sufficient to support the sentence."

It was the necessity for this examination, as well as the advice on clemency requested by General Eisenhower, that resulted in this case's being studied by seven distinguished attorneys.

[182   ]

The army legal authority closest to General Eisenhower, the man who "briefed" the general orally and personally, was his theater judge advocate, Brigadier General Ed. C. Betts. General Betts is dead: he died in Germany shortly after the war ended.

In General Betts's office the chief of the military justice section was Colonel Hardy Hollers, of the law firm of Hollers & O'Quinn, Austin, Texas. Under Colonel Hollers were nine reviewing officers, one of whom was Major Frederick J. Bertolet, presently of Bertolet & Bertolet, Reading, Pennsylvania. After graduating from Harvard Law School in 1935, Major Bertolet represented the Department of Justice of the Commonwealth of Pennsylvania until December, 1941, when he enlisted as a private in the Signal Corps. He was subsequently commissioned and sent to the judge advocate general's school at Ann Arbor, Michigan, after which he went to London and Paris and handled numerous capital cases. He wrote one of the two reviews in the Slovik case — a review which, after being approved by Colonel Hollers and General Betts, was then considered by General Eisenhower.

—— The Slovik case was assigned to me by my section chief as a routine matter, Major Bertolet recalls. When I say routine, you must realize that all of the cases that came to me or to the other junior officers in the military justice section involved death sentences which had already been approved by the appointing authority. While this was exacting and unpleasant duty, the eight other officers and I had become accustomed to it. By that time we all had accumulated experience in these matters.

—— Our offices were located on the top floor of the Hotel Majestic, right off the Etoile. This hotel was the chief building housing Headquarters ETOUSA.

—— My responsibilities, shared with my eight colleagues, were to read and review for legal sufficiency, the cases sent to me to advise my chief whether the rights of the accused had been fully protected at the trial, and, in fact, in all steps of the case — to be certain that the trial was fair; to determine whether or not any psychiatric examination of the accused was adequate and whether any further examination was indicated; to make recommendation as to whether or not clemency should be exercised. It was the duty and responsibility of the reviewing officer to then submit a review to his section chief. If his chief had no criticism, the review went on to General Betts, who would take it personally, with his own comments, to General Eisenhower. In our legal talks, rank meant very little, and independent expression of opinion was encouraged.

—— My primary responsibility was for the correctness of my legal findings. My responsibility on the matter of clemency was secondary, in that at least three higher echelons of officers would review my clemency recommendation; and since it was a personal and not a legal opinion, they were free to reverse or modify my recommendations without consulting me. It would be foolish to say that the recommendation of the reviewing officer and the paragraph on clemency did not carry some weight. In a case such as the Slovik case, however, where the facts were simple and the disposition difficult, the reviewing officer's recommendation on clemency would in no way approach a decisive factor.

—— In the Slovik case no protracted legal discussions were indicated. The record was clean and the facts were clear. The question of guilt never entered into it. General Betts and Colonel Hollers discussed only factual and legal matters with their reviewing officers. On the matter of clemency, they desired the reviewing officers' independent reasoning and judgment. General Betts discussed all of his cases personally with General Eisenhower, but I was not present at their discussion of the Slovik case. General Betts told me, however, that the Slovik case had pained General Eisenhower deeply, as he had longed to equal General Pershing's record in World War I. That was the first time that I learned that no one had been shot for desertion in World War I. I remember at the time that I felt that the relative magnitudes of the armies made comparison rather foolish.

—— No one attempted in any manner to influence

my review. We were dealing with death cases, which was enough of a burden on our consciences as it was. We were left severely alone. I, for one — and, I know, most of my associates — would have requested transfer if interference, direct or indirect, had been permitted. An ordinary judge deals with a few capital cases a year. We were dealing with several a week, and that is a heavy burden on one's heart and soul. We had the right to arrive at our decisions alone and uninfluenced; and this we did.

—— I have no way of knowing to what extent General Eisenhower was influenced by my review. I am sure that he was influenced by the fact that his staff judge advocate, General Betts, concurred in the whole review. General Eisenhower reposed great confidence in General Betts.

—— No, I did not visit Slovik in prison. Not in this case nor in any other case that I know of did the reviewing officer visit the accused. It was the officer's duty to confine himself to the record and the accompanying papers. We found ourselves in a position analogous to that of appellate jurists.

Here are the two sections from Major Bertolet's review, concurred in and personally presented to General Eisenhower by General Betts, which probably were most influential in standing Slovik before the firing squad.

HEADQUARTERS
European Theater of Operations
United States Army

The United States vs. Pvt. Eddie D. Slovik, 36896415.
REVIEW BY STAFF JUDGE ADVOCATE

7. *Discussion* a. The confession by the accused was written by him spontaneously. His desire to confess, in fact, to be tried, was obvious. Even if there were any doubt of the voluntary nature of accused's confession at the time he submitted it on 9 October, the effect and purport of the paper was made clear to him on 11 October and he signed an indorsement re-affirming its voluntary character. While the alleged intent might be inferred from the facts, his confession leaves no possible doubt that both desertions were to avoid hazardous duty within the meaning of Article of War 58. All the elements of both offenses are established beyond any doubt, as accused apparently desired them to be.

9. *Clemency.* The power to exercise clemency is a trust; it is not to be granted as a matter of course in any class of cases, but its exercise should depend upon the facts and considerations of military discipline. The record of the accused in civil life indicates that between 1932 and 1938 he was convicted five times by the Juvenile Court of Detroit for four offenses of breaking and entering and for one instance of assault and battery. In each case he was placed on parole. In 1937 he was sentenced to six months to ten years for embezzlement, and in 1939 he was again confined for unlawfully driving away an automobile. The report of

[187]

the FBI attached to the record does not indicate how much time the accused actually served either in the reformatory or in the state prison, but in his own letter requesting clemency accused states that he was in jail five years. These prior offenses are not of sufficient gravity to influence my recommendation in the instant case. However, they indicate a persistent refusal to conform to the rules of society in civilian life, an imperviousness to penal correction and a total lack of appreciation of clemency; these qualities the accused brought with him into his military life. He was obstinately determined not to engage in combat, and on two occasions, the second after express warning as to results, he deserted. He boldly confessed to these offenses and concluded his confession with the statement, "so I ran away again AND I'LL RUN AWAY AGAIN IF I HAVE TO GO OUT THEIR." There can be no doubt that he deliberately sought the safety and comparative comfort of the guardhouse. To him and to those soldiers who may follow his example, if he achieves his end, confinement is neither deterrent nor punishment. He has directly challenged the authority of the government, and future discipline depends upon a resolute reply to this challenge. If the death penalty is ever to be imposed for desertion it should be imposed in this case, not as a punitive measure nor as retribution, but to maintain that discipline upon which alone an army can succeed against the enemy. There was no recommendation for clemency in this case and *none is here recommended.* [Italics Huie's.]

The important points to note here are these:

1. Major Bertolet — and General Betts — began their paragraph on clemency by striking at the common prac-

tice of extending "automatic" clemency to deserters under death sentence. They said, in effect: "Now wait, General Eisenhower. Clemency is not something to be granted as a matter of course *in any class of cases*. The power to exercise clemency is a trust, and its exercise should depend upon the facts and *considerations of military discipline*." What does this mean? It means that Major Bertolet and General Betts were quite aware of the almost universal assumption that a deserter would not be executed. They knew that Slovik had assumed that he would not be shot. They knew that the members of the court who had passed the sentence on Slovik had assumed that he would not be shot. Major Bertolet and General Betts were convinced that this *assumption* was dangerous to the army and dangerous to the nation, and they saw the Slovik case as an opportunity to end this assumption.

Here is the very heart of the matter. Here is why the Slovik case must become historic. Here is the purpose of this book — to pose *one* question to thoughtful Americans: Is the assumption that an able-bodied citizen can desert the military service of the United States with relative impunity — is this a dangerous assumption? Should it be allowed to prevail? Was the United States at fault in permitting Eddie Slovik — and how many others? — to assume that they could willfully "avoid hazardous duty" at relatively little danger to themselves? Is the United States ready to discard, or seriously modify, the simple soldier's creed expressed by Colonel Rudder: *an able-bodied American who will not fight for his country has no right to live?*

2. A second point to note is that Major Bertolet — and General Betts — pointedly did *not* recommend clemency. This, of course, is not to say that they "urged the death penalty," but was not this the effect? And, in honesty, did they not want an execution in the hope that it would correct an assumption which they regarded as perilous to the nation? Could Major Bertolet and General Betts in honesty have recommended clemency?

3. The third point has to do with whether or not Slovik was the *one* deserter who most deserved to be shot. If *they* had to shoot one man, did they shoot the right one? And here the question is: to what extent did Slovik's civilian record serve to put the finger on him? Note Major Bertolet's handling of this question.

It is of interest that in 1953, when he had not seen his own review for eight years, Major Bertolet replied in this manner to a question about the civilian record:

—— If I did a good job in my review, I must have referred to Slovik's civilian record and indicated whether or not I considered it of any real importance. I am almost sure that the civilian record did not influence me since, as I recall, it showed him to be merely a "bad boy" rather than a confirmed felon. We all had observed that many of these dead-end kids became brave soldiers. Anyway, my theory is that if the army takes a petty criminal and tells him to fight, *it is then unfair and inconsistent to hold his civilian record against him.*

—— Nothing could be more absurd than the statement to McKendrick attributed to Slovik. ["They are shooting me for bread I stole when I was twelve years old."] Nothing could be further from the truth. Remember that the court that convicted him of the gravest of war crimes knew nothing of his record before they found him guilty.

But here Major Bertolet would seem to be missing the principal point. What makes this case distinctive is not that Private Slovik was *sentenced* to be shot for desertion. Many other deserters share that distinction, *all* of whom were granted clemency. What makes Eddie Slovik unique is that he was the only deserter sentenced to be shot *to whom clemency was not extended.* And the men responsible for not extending clemency to Slovik were Colonel Sommer, General Cota, Major Bertolet, Colonel Hollers, General Betts, Major Stevens, Colonel Sargent, General Riter, General McNeil, and General Eisenhower.

These are the Americans, more so than the members of the court, who share the responsibility, in varying degree, for the actual shooting of Slovik. They denied him clemency and ordered him shot for high, threefold purpose: 1) to correct a dangerous assumption, 2) as a deterrent, and 3) as deserved punishment for a confessed crime. And all of these Americans knew of the civilian record; each of them, in varying degree, may have been influenced by it.

So was Slovik being entirely "absurd" when he concluded that he was being shot "for bread I stole when I was twelve years old"? And to the extent that they were influenced by the civilian record, were not at least some of these reviewing authorities violating the forthright theory stated by Major Bertolet: if the army takes a petty criminal and tells him to fight, it is then unfair and inconsistent to hold his civilian record against him?

Eddie Slovik is not on trial here; he is dead. For the high purpose of clarification and national understanding, the men on trial here are those who conferred great distinction on Private Slovik. Should they have shot a deserter for these purposes, and should Slovik have been the one?

4

The other legal reviewing authority in Paris — the highest one . . . the one charged with the responsibility of satisfying Article of War 50½ . . . the one which, before the sentence could be executed, had to inform General Eisenhower that "the record of trial has been examined and found legally sufficient to support the sentence" — was the branch office of the judge advocate

[192   ]

general with the European Theater of Operations . . . and this office was headed by Brigadier General E. C. McNeil, Assistant Judge Advocate General.

General McNeil, who has all the judicial dignity of a Charles Evans Hughes, has devoted a lifetime to military law. A native of Minnesota, West Point Class of '07, he was one of the first four officers to be sent to law school by the army — another member of that group of four was the late General Hugh "Blue Eagle" Johnson. He graduated in law from Columbia in 1916, and was chief clemency adviser to General Pershing in and after the First War. Now retired, he lives in Washington, where he is an elder in the National Presbyterian Church and a frequent civilian adviser at the Pentagon.

General McNeil is a merciful man: he earned the reputation of leaning over backward to favor the accused. And he is a scrapper. One of the Pentagon legends is about how he induced the late Judge Patterson, when secretary of war, to override General Eisenhower and return to duty a young lieutenant who had refused an order, under dramatic circumstances, from his battalion commander.

Under General McNeil in Paris, the Board of Review Number One was headed by Brigadier General Franklin Riter, a reserve officer, of Salt Lake City, Utah; and the other two members of this board were Colonel Ellwood W. Sargent, now with the Regular Army in

Japan, and Major Edward L. Stevens, Jr., of New York, now a lieutenant colonel, a reserve officer, who in 1953 was on active duty in Japan.

In the Slovik case Major Stevens wrote the basic draft of the review, which is signed by himself, Colonel Sargent, and General Riter, and to which there is appended an endorsement, with comment, by General McNeil.

Here, first, are the 1953 recollections of Colonel Stevens, written from Japan:

—— It was no part of my function to pass on the appropriateness of Slovik's sentence, only on the legality. I recall the case as one of the two most aggravated desertion cases that came to my attention during World War II, particularly because the accused deliberately sought safe incarceration in preference to doing his soldier's job.

—— I am not in favor of capital punishment except in extreme cases. I regarded the Slovik case as an extreme one, and my recollection is that most of those with whom I talked about it felt as I did. The thing that highlighted this case was the fact that the death penalty had not been executed for a purely military offense for a great many years. I feel there is at least as much chance that this was wrong as that Slovik's execution was wrong.

—— The view was expressed that if *seriously aggravated* desertions had been punished by the death sentence early in the war, there would have been far fewer desertions. I'm inclined to agree with this.

———This undoubtedly sounds hard to Americans who reside far from battle lines. It is hard. War, unfortunately, is a hard business. When you take troops into battle you must have discipline, and you cannot tolerate or condone aggravated, deliberate desertion. Desertions vary greatly in seriousness, and if you don't punish each desertion case *according to its own merits*, your army is bound to suffer. The acid test of the combat soldier is his performance in combat. The soldier who with calculated deliberation chooses to shirk combat, thereby increasing the burden on his fellows, should be punished so severely that others will be dissuaded from following his example.

———I do not mean to imply that the utmost caution should not be exercised before a soldier is ordered executed for a purely military offense. But I do firmly believe that some aggravated desertions require the death penalty and that Slovik's was one of them.

———The hue and cry which followed the news of Slovik's execution indicate that many people don't share my views. Probably some of them knew all the facts of the case. Undoubtedly a large proportion of them did not and still do not. I shall observe with interest the reaction to full publication.

———You will understand, of course, that the views expressed here are strictly my own personal views, and

[195   ]

I do not purport to speak for the defense department, the army, or the JAG Corps.

The important conclusions in the body of the review are these:

Careful and painstaking examination of the record of trial reveals that accused was accorded fully due process of law as provided by the Articles of War, and fails to show any action, or ruling by the trial court which prejudiced in any degree the substantial rights of the accused. Eleven days elapsed between the service of charges upon him and the date of trial at which defense counsel specifically stated that accused was "ready to proceed with the trial at this time." The voluntariness of his confession is attested by the evident fact that he himself wrote it on the flower order form and signed it wholly on his own initiative before submitting it to military authorities. Under the circumstances it constituted a particularly credible and damning piece of evidence, as accused obviously intended it should be. . . . There is nothing in the record of trial to indicate that accused was other than sane and responsible for his acts either at the time of the offenses or at the time of trial. The statement of the division neuropsychiatrist dated 26 October 1944, and contained in the accompanying papers, is an affirmative indication of accused's sanity and responsibility at those times.

And here is General McNeil's comment in his endorsement:

This is the first death sentence for desertion which has reached me for examination. It is probably the first of the kind in the American Army for over eighty years — there were none in World War I. In this case the extreme penalty of death appears warranted. This soldier had performed no front line duty. He did not intend to. He deserted from his group of fifteen when about to join the infantry company to which he had been assigned. His subsequent conduct shows a deliberate plan to secure trial and incarceration in a safe place. *The sentence adjudged was more severe than he had anticipated,* but the imposition of a less severe sentence would only have accomplished the accused's purpose of securing his incarceration and consequent freedom from the dangers which so many of our armed forces are required to face daily. *His unfavorable civilian record indicates that he is not a worthy subject of clemency.* [Italics Huie's.]

There is the final word on the civilian record. Colonel Sommer began the reviewing process with the attitude: "I didn't think they would execute a deserter, but I thought that if ever they wanted a horrible example this was one."

General McNeil ended the reviewing process by saying: "His unfavorable civilian record indicates that he is not a worthy subject of clemency."

Major Bertolet's theory is: "If the army takes a petty criminal and tells him to fight, it is then unfair and inconsistent to hold his civilian record against him."

Do these statements indicate that Eddie Slovik may have been the *one* deserter who was shot because he was the *one* who had stolen bread when he was twelve years old?

[197   ]

The last two entries on General Court-Martial Order No. 27 are:

Record of trial examined by the Board of Review with the concurrence of the Assistant Judge Advocate General, Branch Office of TJAG with ETO, and found legally sufficient to support the sentence.

Signed: B. Franklin Riter
Chairman, Board of Review

The sentence having been modified and approved by the convening authority, confirmed by the Commanding General, European Theater of Operations, and Article of War 50½ having been complied with, will be carried into execution on 31 January 1945, at 109th Infantry Area, France. The act of execution will be under the direction of the Provost Marshal, 28th Infantry Division.

By command of General Eisenhower:
R. B. LORD
Major General, GSC, Deputy Chief
of Staff

Official Seal: R. B. LOVETT
Brigadier General, USA,
Adjutant General

Ten . . .

Except that it is much smaller, the little mountain town of St. Marie aux Mines in eastern France is like Scranton, Pennsylvania, home of the 109th Infantry. The mines are coal mines. It's a community of eight or ten thousand, the houses set down along a swift, black stream, with hills rearing up in every back yard. The snow is deep in January, and the coal dust settles on the snow . . . like Scranton. The people are like mountain folk everywhere: phlegmatic, inured to struggle — they send their children out to wave at all invading armies.

The invaders during the last days of January, 1945, were Americans . . . the 28th Division. Many of the best houses had been commandeered. The division was busy: preparing to launch the Colmar offensive.

St. Marie had been marked for distinction. Here, on January 31st, the United States was going to try to correct what had been adjudged a perilous assumption — the assumption that an American soldier could refuse to fight without jeopardizing his life. Here, a long, long way from Ionia, the people of the United States were going to make an example of Private Eddie D. Slovik.

The order came through from Paris on January 24th . . . to General Cota, thence to the office of the provost marshal — the 28th's chief of police — Major William Fellman, 2nd, of Philadelphia. Fellman, by order of General Eisenhower, would be in charge. He would be assisted by Lieutenant Zygmont E. Koziak, who would handle the firing squad. Other assistants would be two stout sergeants, James W. Hess and Frank J. McKendrick, Philadelphia, who would guard the accused, bind him to the post.

Fellman, Koziak, Hess and McKendrick — they were the personnel in charge of arrangements. They'd select the site, assemble the cast, await the delivery of the prisoner from Paris, execute the will of the United States.

But what was the Standard Operating Procedure — the SOP — for such an execution? The last time the people of the United States had shot a coward "to death with musketry," muskets had been used . . . in the snows of northern Virginia. So Major Fellman's first act was to telephone army headquarters to rush him the SOP — SOP No. 54: Execution of Death Sentences Imposed by Courts-Martial.

Preliminary Preparations. a. The place of execution will

[200   ]

be prepared to provide for a back wall made of absorbent material, before which the prisoner will be placed. An upright post will be placed in front of the back wall and will be used to support the prisoner if necessary.

The entire area around St. Marie was surveyed for the best site. At first it was decided to use an open field, under a hill, to accommodate the maximum number of troop witnesses. But this idea was discarded when it was decided that the execution must be kept secret from French civilians. Theretofore, in executing the murderers and rapists, such secrecy had been thought not necessary: civilians had been involved in most of those crimes, so those prisoners were hanged, usually in the communities in which the crimes were committed, and civilian witnesses were welcomed . . . to witness an act of faith. But the Slovik case was different: no civilian had been involved, only the United States and Private Slovik, so no Frenchman should learn that the United States was dealing so drastically with its "desertion problem."

On January 27th the perfect site was found: *86 Rue de Général Dourgeois.* On the northern outskirts of St. Marie was a house and garden almost out of melodrama. A three-story gray house with orange shutters. You approached it by stopping your jeep short of the mountain stream which rushed, moatlike, in front of it . . . then walking over a footbridge, opening tall iron gates. Behind the house was a garden which, like the entire

[201]

property, was enclosed by a high masonry wall; and rising on two sides of the garden were snow-covered hills.

In the precise report of Major Fellman:

The following facts influenced our selecting #86 Rue de General Dourgeois: The location was not adjacent to any town activity. A very important factor was that a stone wall approximately 7½' high surrounded the property. The property was secured via Military Government. The occupants did not know for what purpose it was to be used. The occupants were asked to vacate the premises two days prior to the execution as were occupants of any of the nearby properties that commanded a view of the scene of execution. A security guard was established 24 hours prior to the execution, and all possible points of view were cut off to both civilian and military personnel. Both prior to the execution and afterwards the entire matter was kept from the civilian populace.

On the morning of January 30th, as soon as the property was controlled and blacked-out by MPs, the assistant division engineer, Captain Robert J. Hummel, Philadelphia, moved in with a detail "to provide for a back wall made of absorbent material, before which the prisoner will be placed." The carpenters, using heavy boards several inches thick, built a barrier six feet high and six feet wide, standing parallel with — and about three feet away from — the masonry wall. The barrier was to serve as a "ricochet board": a bullet could pass through Slovik's body and, if it didn't hit the six-inch-thick post, it could penetrate the board, strike the stone wall, and perhaps ricochet against the board without danger to the firing squad and witnesses. A bullet from an M-1 rifle will kill a man at two miles, so fired from twenty paces and striking a stone wall it can be a wild and fearsome thing.

Captain Hummel's men also "placed the upright post in front of the back wall . . . a post to be used to support the prisoner if necessary." They dug through the snow and into the frozen ground and implanted a six by six which stood six feet high. Into the back of the post, at shoulder level, was driven "a large spike-type nail to support the straps after the shooting when the body slumps."

The carpenters devised one other apparatus required by the SOP:

If while the condemned is being prepared for, or marched to, the place of execution, collapse has taken place or is imminent, a suitable braceboard and straps will be adjusted.

It was assumed that since Slovik was a condemned coward he probably would not be able to walk out to the post and stand there while the order was being read to him. So a "collapse board" was fashioned, with straps, on which he could be carried out and stood up against the post to hear the order and receive the volley.

[203]

Captain Hummel's detail completed its work by digging paths in the snow: a path leading to the post, to be used by the "execution procession," and paths for the firing squad and witnesses.

Major N. B. Thompson, the division military government officer, completed the physical preparations for the execution by satisfying this SOP requirement:

A hood of thick black cloth, loose fitting, to cover the head and neck of the prisoner and to obscure all light, will be provided.

Major Thompson purchased the black cloth in St. Marie and engaged a local seamstress to make the hood. Major Fellman states: "Neither the person from whom the material was secured nor the seamstress knew for what purpose it was to be used."

2

The personnel specified by the SOP for such an execution — other than the MPs and the firing squad — include three medical officers, a chaplain, a recorder, a representative of the corps or army to which the division is attached, and not less than five officially designated military witnesses.

The three doctors assigned to the Slovik execution were Major Robert E. Rougelot, of New Orleans, Captain Marion B. Davis, Jr., and Captain Charles E. Galt.

Dr. Rougelot, the senior examiner, is six feet three inches tall, weighs two hundred pounds, and wears a mustache: he is a thoughtful man, an impressive-looking figure.

—— I was intimately acquainted with all the officers concerned with the execution, he recalls. The general feeling was one of deadly seriousness, and the officers were all acutely desirous of carrying out the harrowing assignment exactly as prescribed. On the afternoon of January 30th, when the firing squad was rehearsed, I was asked to instruct the squad as to the position of the heart. The members of the squad filed silently into a room adjacent to the courtyard. I selected a man about the size and height of Slovik and pointed out the outline of the heart. Someone suggested pinning a piece of paper the size of the heart over Slovik's heart before the actual shooting, but somehow I felt such a procedure would tend toward the theatrical, so I suggested that a good marksman at such a short distance should be able to strike the area outlined.

—— None of the riflemen had any questions, and I was impressed with their seriousness. The job, obviously, was most distasteful to them.

The chaplain who was summoned to division headquarters to attend Private Slovik is legendary with the 109th. Father Carl Patrick Cummings, now rector of St. Patrick's Church, Nicholson, Pennsylvania — about twenty miles north of Scranton. My wife and I sat on his front porch with him one Saturday afternoon in August, and talked. I had found him painting signs in his recreation room, getting ready for a Saturday-night kids' party. He gave me a jolt of Four Roses to cut the dust in my throat.

"I'm proud to have been one of the first Americans to spit tobacco juice on those dragons' teeth in the Siegfried Line," he said.

If Eddie Slovik met Strength of one variety in General Cota, he met still another variety in Father Cummings. For the father is a real combat priest — a latter-day Friar Tuck, equally proficient with a Bible or a barrel stave. A modest, gentle, but muscular little man, he dodged as much lead as any soldier in the 28th Division. And the reluctant lads got little sympathy from him.

"One day," he said, "we were under fire in Hürtgen, and a rifleman came up to me and said, 'Father, I'm lucky. I haven't had to shoot my rifle yet.' I almost blew my top. 'How many lads have been shot giving you protection?' I asked him. 'How many have got hurt giving away their positions to save your neck? Man, using your rifle here is your duty, both to yourself and to your outfit.' "

Father Cummings, too, is a proud inheritor, a resolute defender of the faith. His unquestioning devotions are to the Blessed Lord, the United States of America, the

[206]

Holy Roman Catholic Church, the 109th Infantry Regiment, and the Ould Sod.

"My grandfather came here with a tag around his neck," he told me. "It's a great, wonderful country, worth protecting — that's why I'm an isolationist."

—— I, of course, had never met Eddie Slovik, the father recalls. I was ordered back to St. Marie on the morning of January 30th in order to be there when he was delivered to us. We expected the MPs from Paris to deliver him during the evening of January 30th, and I was prepared to spend the night with him. But the MPs were delayed by the snowstorm and didn't arrive until about 7:30 A.M. on the 31st. I met the boys in the firing squad during the afternoon of the 30th. Since I was chaplain of the 109th, they were all "my boys" and they knew me. They were disturbed. None of them had any stomach for the job. Some of them told me they hated to have to shoot one of their own.

—— I gave them what assurance I could. I told them that higher authority had assumed the moral responsibility for Eddie Slovik's death . . . that this authority was not theirs to question . . . that they should perform their assignment to the best of their ability.

The official recorder for the execution was Colonel Sommer, the division judge advocate who had offered to help Slovik if he would try to serve in the line . . . and who had not recommended that General Cota extend clemency.

[207]

Here is the SOP requirement for a firing squad:

Firing Squad. A firing squad in charge of a sergeant, consisting of not less than eight and not more than twelve enlisted men skilled in the use of the regulation rifle, will be selected by the officer designated to carry out the act of execution. These soldiers will be made available, duly ordered by name to comprise the firing squad, and will carry out the duties assigned to them as members thereof.

When the hood has been adjusted and signal given that the prisoner is in final readiness, the firing squad will be marched by the sergeant to a designated spot and formed in single or double rank facing the prisoner and not less than twenty paces from him. The members of the firing squad will be armed with regulation rifles, each of which will have been loaded and the pieces locked by the officer charged with the execution of the sentence. One of the rifles will contain a blank round, and the identity of this piece will not be disclosed. Each of the remaining rifles will contain one round of service ammunition.

The officer charged with the execution of the sentence will take over the firing squad and command: 1. Squad, 2. Ready, 3. Aim, 4. Fire. At the command "FIRE" each member of the firing squad will discharge his piece point-blank at the prisoner's heart. If, in the opinion of the medical officers, the prisoner has not sustained a mortal wound, the rifles will be reloaded and the procedure outlined herein will be repeated until there is inflicted a mortal wound from which extinction of life is immediately imminent.

By command of General Eisenhower

On January 28th General Cota named the members of the firing squad in this order:

SPECIAL ORDERS
NUMBER 17
The following listed EM are detailed for duty as members of the firing squad to execute the sentence of death by shooting imposed by a General Court-Martial upon Pvt. Eddie D. Slovik 36896415 Co "G" 109th Inf. EM will report for duty to the Director of the Execution at the Office of the Provost Marshal, this hq, at [a] time specified by the Director of the Execution:

Sgt Albert H. Bruns	36027946	Co "F", 109th — IN COMMAND
Pvt Aaron Morrison	35656274	Hq Co, 1st Bn, 109th
Pvt James K. Baker	35132803	Co "A", 109th
Pfc Oscar R. Kittle	33607832	Co "D", 109th
Pfc Earl J. Williams	33366036	Co "B", 109th
Pvt John R. James	35815616	Co "F", 109th
Pvt Clarence M. Revlet	35815637	Co "F", 109th
Pvt Robert A. Irons	37644124	Co "G", 109th
Pvt Charles E. McDaniel	34936344	Co "G", 109th
Pfc Trinidad Sanchez	36266351	Hq Co, 3d Bn, 109th
Pvt Cass W. Carper	36455522	Hq Co, 3d Bn, 109th
Pvt Frank Nawrocki	12182922	Hq Co, 3d Bn, 109th
Pvt Thomas E. Keresey	31264843	Hq Co, 3d Bn, 109th

By command of Major General Cota

These men were picked by Colonel Rudder on the basis of being expert riflemen. All three battalions of the regiment were represented. At the suggestion of the army's Office of Public Information, the members of the firing squad will not be identified here with their present home addresses. The sole exception will be Private Morrison, whose home is in West Virginia, and who will be quoted as a representative spokesman for the group.

Here are Morrison's recollections up to the evening of January 30th:

—— I remember everything that happened very clearly, even to the remarks that were made.

—— I was drafted March 29, 1943, at Huntington, West Virginia, when I was eighteen. My father was a schoolteacher. He was killed in an automobile wreck July 8, 1938. I was working in a coal-company store, supporting my mother, when I was drafted. I was single at the time; I married in 1952. I'm twenty-eight now; I was twenty at the time of the firing squad. I joined the 28th Division as a replacement in France, and was with the 109th all the way. I was in three major battles: Ardennes, Rhineland and Central Europe. I was a marksman with the M-1 rifle, carbine, light thirty machine gun, and expert bayonet and forty-five automatic. I qualified with the BAR and bazooka.

—— I was a messenger between battalion headquarters and company. I was in the open all the time, with no hole to jump into when things started happening. I guided mule teams loaded with ammo and rations to the companies in the Vosges Mountains. This was interesting if you lived long enough. French Moroccans owned the mules. This was the only way of getting supplies to the companies. All nightwork. You couldn't come out in the daytime and live.

——— I did not have any use for a deserter. No one in my company took off. I did not know Slovik personally . . . never saw him until we marched into the courtyard and he was strapped to the post with a black hood over his head. I never heard him mentioned until I learned I was on the firing squad.

——— Yes, I remember what was said when we learned there was going to be a firing squad. The first sergeant informed me I was elected to the job around ten o'clock in the morning . . . that would be the 29th. My buddy, Lambert, and four or five other boys were present. We were playing poker. That was the end of the game. Everybody was on his feet and asking the sarge questions at the same time. I thought for a minute that he had cracked up for sure, and then I saw he was serious.

——— Old Lambert spoke up and said: "What the hell they need those eleven other guys for? Old Pappy here ain't missed a squirrel's head at a hundred yards since he was six years old! Those other guys'll just be wasting ammunition." Pappy was my nickname.

——— I couldn't quite believe it so I took off to see the captain. I asked him if there was any way to get out of the firing-squad deal. His reply was: "Not unless you want to take his place." That didn't appeal to me. So some of the boys and I had a bull session, and we decided he had it coming to him. He had deserted us when he was needed most, and his leaving could have caused a whole company of good men to have been slaughtered by Jerry patrols, of which there was plenty running around loose.

—— The reason I was picked, so I was told, was that they had picked twelve of the best shots in the regiment. Some said they picked us because we were always taking long chances and were inclined to be a little "trigger happy."

—— That afternoon, the 29th, the firing squad left regimental headquarters for division headquarters and the place of execution. We were riding in a six by six truck. I didn't know any other member of the squad, as they were from different companies, and we were all strangers to each other. There was not too much talk. They were hooked and they knew they couldn't get out of it.

—— When we arrived at Division we were given a pep talk by Lieutenant Koziak. He just told us what we had to do and there was nothing to feel bad about. Next morning, January 30th, we were paid a visit by General Cota himself, and he told us to be sure that our aim was good and to make one shot do the job and not mess it up. He also gave us a briefing about Slovik's past criminal record. As he left I heard him remark to a colonel

[212]

that was with him that we were a regular bunch of GIs and that there was nothing to worry about.

—— That afternoon we had the rehearsal. Lieutenant Koziak was in charge. We tramped around in that deep snow, and had a "dry run" at the target. We went in the house and Dr. Rougelot talked to us, gave us detailed information of where to aim to hit the heart. He stood one of the boys up and outlined where to shoot.

—— We also saw Chaplain Cummings that afternoon. We all knew him. He was our 109th chaplain, and he had come back to be with Slovik. He was a rough and tumble chaplain: all the time up on the front lines. I thought he'd get shot every day, but for some reason he didn't. We talked to the chaplain that afternoon and told him we had tried to get out of the firing squad, but he said we shouldn't feel bad, that the decision had been made by our superiors, and that we had a job to do.

This manner in which the firing squad was handled is one of the most revealing aspects of the Slovik case . . . revealing as to the nature of our times. There was uncertainty, almost anxiety, among the division command, including General Cota, over how a firing squad would perform in such a case.

These twelve youngsters share a considerable distinction: they are the only Americans in the twentieth century who have been called upon by their nation to kill a fellow citizen for a "crime" of omission.

Eddie Slovik is the only American to be executed since 1864 for the crime of *avoiding* a duty!

In 1945 . . . in the Age of Freud . . . in the age of excuse for individual failure — could twelve American youngsters be depended on to kill one of their fellows for failing? No one could be certain; it just hadn't been tried in "modern times." Those were uncomplicated days back in 1863 in northern Virginia; that was a Brothers' War; men had different ideas about failure then. But in 1945 could American youths, who had been taught that a man's shortcomings might not be his own fault — could they be trusted to shoot the heart out of a fellow who was guilty, not of any crime of violence . . . not of murder or rape or treason . . . but only of a crime of refusal to undertake a hazardous duty?

Suppose the first volley was fired and all the eleven bullets hit the baffle board and none hit Private Slovik? The rifles would be reloaded and a second volley would be fired. Suppose again, for all the expert marksmanship of the firing squad, there were eleven clean misses? The SOP made no provision for this. Nobody quite believed it could happen, but how, after an interval of eighty-two years in a nation's history, could one be sure?

The systematic effort to make sure this didn't happen began with the selection of the firing squad by Colonel Rudder. He picked his most reliable "combative types." They were sent to division headquarters two days before the execution. There were talks by Lieutenant Koziak;

firing instruction by Dr. Rougelot; a rehearsal at the site to familiarize the riflemen with the machinery of execution — the post, the ricochet board, the collapse board; and then the talks by General Cota and Father Cummings.

General Cota made two personal appearances before the firing squad: one on the morning of January 30th, and again only a few minutes before the execution. In his first appearance the General spoke of Slovik's "criminal civilian record." Why? Was he saying in effect: "Boys, if you feel any hesitancy about shooting this criminal for his crime of failing to perform a duty, let me remind you that he is also a more conventional sort of criminal"? All these references to the civilian record carried implications that it was the sort that twenty-year-old Americans in 1945 could more readily accept as being worthy of death.

Father Cummings was the anchor man of the indoctrination team. On January 30th, in his talk with the firing squad, he told them to do their duty . . . that the decision to shoot Slovik was not theirs to question . . . that the responsibility for Slovik's death had been assumed by higher authority.

4

There was a snowstorm throughout most of eastern France during the evening and on into the night of January 30, 1945. And through that swirling snow a beam of light might, briefly, have illuminated these four scenes:

At his chateau in St. Marie, Lieutenant General Frank W. "Shrimp" Milburn gave a dinner that evening. He commanded the XXIst Army Corps, which next day would launch the Colmar offensive. The 28th and 3rd Divisions had been attached to this corps. The dinner was for generals: among those present were General Jacob Devers, Major General Faye B. Prickett, and Brigadier Generals Ward H. Maris and Rinaldo Van Brunt.

There were two officers present who were not generals: Colonel Edward L. R. Elson, the ranking chaplain of the XXIst Corps, and Lieutenant Colonel Henry Cabot Lodge, who now heads the United States delegation to the United Nations.

Colonel Elson, a Pennsylvanian, had considered going to West Point before finally deciding to become a Presbyterian minister. He now presides over the National Presbyterian Church, Washington, D.C., where his congregation includes President Eisenhower, General McNeil, and John Edgar Hoover.

Near the end of the dinner General Milburn turned to Colonel Elson and said: "Chaplain, tomorrow morning the 28th Division is executing a private soldier by firing squad for desertion. I wish you would attend as my representative and give me a full report."

[216]

Somewhere in the Vosges Mountains a weapons carrier from Paris, delayed by the snow, had halted at a
farmhouse which had been commandeered by Americans and where coffee and food were available. Two
MPs got out, went inside and ate, then came back and
relieved the other two MPs so that they could go in and
eat. The fifth man didn't get out: he sat in the back
seat in handcuffs and with his ankles bound.

The first two MPs had brought him sandwiches and
a can of coffee. They unlocked his handcuffs so he could
eat. He wasn't hungry, but as he sat there trying to eat,
he said:

"Come on, fellows, and give me a break. Untie my
feet and let me run out there in the snow. You shoot
me with your carbines and get it over with."

"No, Eddie," one of them replied, "you're a good guy,
but we can't do that. They got a big party planned for
you over in St. Marie . . . the full-dress treatment. After
they get through with you, these dogfaces are supposed to think twice before they take off. Just relax and
drink your coffee; it won't be long."

PRIVATE MORRISON: After the rehearsal all of us in the
firing squad had chow together, and then we went to
the house where we were billeted. We all bunked together. There was some nervousness that night. We sat
there and talked. Nobody said anything about injustice:
we all figured Slovik had it coming to him. But some of

[217   ]

the boys sure wished they could get out of the job, and hated to go through with it. They said they might aim high: they just didn't know what they'd do.

—— "I hope I don't have to live the rest of my life thinking it was my bullet that killed him," one boy said.

—— "Yeah," another one said, "it's bad enough to have to kill these goddam krauts, much less one of our own."

—— But another little guy was real tough. He said: "I got no sympathy for the sonofabitch! He deserted us, didn't he? He didn't give a damn how many of us got the hell shot out of us, why should we care about him? I'll shoot his goddam heart out. If only one shot hits him, you'll know it's mine."

—— I personally figured that Slovik was a no-good, and that what he had done was as bad as murder. I was sorry I had been picked, but my mind was settled: my shot wouldn't be high ... and I could hit a dime at that distance. We all turned in, and I don't believe much sleep was lost that night by any of us. I slept all right.

At the quarters of the provost marshal, Major Fellman and Father Cummings were bunking together that night. Fellman was worried over whether the MPs from Paris would get through the snow, and Father Cummings was ready to get up at any hour and spend the rest of the night with Slovik. The father had twenty-eight letters from Antoinette to give him, and he hoped he'd have time to read them. The night wore on, and the two men shifted on their cots and talked.

—— I never knew Fellman very well before then, Father Cummings said to me. But that night — and later — we came to know one another pretty well. Like Herod and Pilate.

5

Except for brief explanatory paragraphs the events between 7:30 and 10:30 A.M., January 31, 1945, will be detailed here through the recollections of eight Americans who were there: Major Fellman, Sergeant Mc-Kendrick, Private Morrison, Father Cummings, Chaplain Elson, Captain Hummel, Dr. Rougelot, and General Cota.

MAJOR FELLMAN: At 7:30 A.M. the MPs from Paris finally arrived with Private Slovik at my office near the center of St. Marie. The corporal in charge, head of the four-man detail, explained that they had been delayed by the snowstorm. He also said that the key to Slovik's handcuffs had been lost, presumably when the detail halted for chow sometime during the night. I signed for the prisoner. Present in my office at the time the prisoner arrived were Father Cummings, Lieutenant Colonel Hoban, Lieutenants Hucker and Koziak, Sergeants Hess and McKendrick, and my clerk, Corporal Elliott. We removed Slovik's handcuffs with a hacksaw.

... I immediately read the prisoner the entire General Court-Martial Orders, informed him that he would be shot by a firing squad at 1000 hours that day, and asked him if he had any special requests. He answered no. I then asked him if he desired the services of Father Cummings. He replied that he did. Slovik was exceptionally calm and resigned throughout my conversation with him. . . . He was bareheaded, wore regulation shoes, wool pants and shirt, and a field jacket — no insignia.

SERGEANT MCKENDRICK: Apparently the MPs from Paris had become rather friendly with him during the long ride in the snowstorm. They told me that he had propositioned them several times to let him run and be shot. I guess most of us would rather get it running than standing at a post.

PRIVATE MORRISON: Man, it was blue cold that morning. Snow knee-deep. It had stopped snowing, but it was overcast, looked like it might start snowing again any time. All of us in the firing squad was cold and tense, even while we was having chow together.

FATHER CUMMINGS: Eddie turned to me and said: "Father, are you a priest? Then can I go to confession and mass?" I told him that I was a priest, that he had about two hours, that I would be with him every minute, and that every comfort the Catholic Church had to offer on such an occasion he could have. . . . We then moved by truck to the house at the execution site, and the MPs took Eddie and me into a room on the first floor. They took the handcuffs off Eddie and left us alone together while they guarded the windows and door. I set up the altar. I was assisted by my server, young Private Zealon H. White, of Los Angeles: he later carried the "collapse board" in the execution procession. I heard Eddie's confession and gave him Absolution while he said an Act of Contrition:

. . . . I absolve thee from thy sins in the name of the Father, and of the Son, and of the Holy Ghost. Amen.

. . . . O my God, I am heartily sorry for having offended Thee, and I detest all my sins. . . .

—— I suggested that he say a Rosary, and he said, "Father, I don't know it all, will you help me?" I nodded, told him to answer the Our Fathers, the Hail Marys, and the Glory Bes, and I would help with the rest. Then I offered mass for him.

—— When we had finished with the religious service, I gave him the bundle of letters from his wife, and he sat there and read several of them, and I noticed him wipe a tear or two as he read. "The only break I ever had in life, Father," he said, "was this girl. But I've lost her now. Everything we had will be gone. They wouldn't let us be happy."

—— I said to him, "Son, the decision in your case is not ours to question. This is war. The moral responsibility for your death has been accepted for the people of the United States of America. Today I want you to walk out there and die with courage."

—— "Will you be with me, Father?" he asked.

—— "I'll be there."

—— "Then I'm all right," he said. "And, Father, I want you to tell the fellows in the regiment that Eddie Slovik wasn't a coward — at least not today."

—— "I'll tell them, Eddie."

—— He sat there thoughtfully for a few minutes, then he said: "Father, I'm getting a break that the fellows up on the line don't get. Here I get to sit here with you and I know I'm going to get it. I *know* I'm going to die in a few minutes. But up there on the line you never know when it's coming, and it's that uncertainty that gets you. I guess that's what I couldn't take — that uncertainty."

—— He asked me about the firing squad, and I told him the boys didn't like the job . . . that they were good guys. "Then before we go out, Father," he said, "you be sure to tell them that I don't hold it against them, and please shoot straight so I won't have to suffer."

Colonel Elson: I arrived at Number Eighty-six Rue de Général Dourgeois about 9 a.m. I had traveled there in a command car with a party which included Lieutenant Colonel William H. Ellsworth, provost marshal of the Third Infantry Division; Lieutenant Colonel Ralph E. Smith, a chaplain, a Catholic, from San Antonio, Texas, of the Third Division; Major Lloyd E. Langford, a chaplain, of the Third Division; and Captain K. M. Bigelow and Sergeant Robert L. Broward, both of the XXIst Corps MP platoon. The Third Division was particularly interested in the Slovik execution since they had an execution pending, but which, for some reason, was never actually consummated.

—— That estate where the execution occurred was out of fiction. The gardens must have been beautiful in season. I remarked that the creek was like a moat as we walked across the bridge, through the big iron gates, and up to the house, where MPs checked our credentials and let us into a large reception room on the second floor. Fifteen, maybe twenty, officers were standing about, visiting gravely and quietly in twos and threes. I remember meeting Colonel Sommer: he was carrying the black hood. I knew General Cota only slightly, but I recognized him standing there in the center of the room: he carried a swagger stick with a brass handle. He spoke to me and asked when I was going to get him some more chaplains: he had lost about a third of his chaplains in the Battle of the Bulge. I told him I was doing my best.

—— The mood in the room was solemn, very serious. We stayed there until about nine-forty-five when it was suggested that we move out into the garden.

PRIVATE MORRISON: I guess we got up to the house about nine-fifteen. They drove us up there in a truck.

We all carried our rifles: each man had brought his own rifle. Since I normally carried a carbine in my work in the mountains, I had had to borrow an M-1, and I had borrowed one from a cook. That was a mistake, for you probably know that no cook ever cleaned his rifle. . . . We assembled in a back room on the ground floor, and General Cota came in and gave us a short talk. He said he was depending on us to do our duty, that we were the finest marksmen in the army and that he wanted us to shoot straight and he knew we could do it. . . . Then we gave our rifles to Lieutenant Koziak and he took them in another room to load them.

MAJOR FELLMAN: The twelve rifles were placed on a large table — oblong dining-room type. Koziak and I loaded the rifles. One blank was employed. We shuffled the rifles around so that neither Koziak nor I knew where the blank was. We had locked them. Then each member of the firing squad came in and claimed his own rifle by number.

(This one-blank business, devised a century or so ago to leave a reasonable doubt in the mind of every rifleman as to whether he had actually participated in the killing, has been made largely meaningless by technical development. The M-1, being a high-powered rifle, not a musket, kicks like a mule when a live round is fired offhand; but there is almost no recoil from a blank.

[224   ]

Moreover, the M-1 automatically ejects the shell of a live round, while it will not eject the shell of a blank. So there was little question among this firing squad as to who drew the blank — and it wasn't Private Morrison.)

COLONEL ELSON: As we officer-witnesses* moved out of the house we assembled informally in two ranks, facing the post and the ricochet board, and standing about two paces back of the line where the firing squad would stand. I recall that there were about a dozen of us, six in each rank. As the highest-ranking witness I remember I stood first in line at the right in the front rank. Ralph Smith stood next to me. The enlisted-men witnesses † were drawn up formally to our left. The

---

* These officer-witnesses did not include either the officers who were officiating in the execution or the officers of the 28th Division, who stood in another position with General Cota. The officer-witnesses were:

Col	Edward L. R. Elson	0276662	Hq XXI Corps
Lt Col	Ralph J. Smith	0387339	Hq 3rd Inf Div
Lt Col	Wm. H. Ellsworth	0318424	Hq 3rd Inf Div
Major	Lloyd E. Langford	0349150	Hq 3rd Inf Div
Major	James K. Watts	0314309	Hq 3rd Inf Div
Capt	Sergiue P. Peachin	0516932	Co D, 103rd Med Bn
Capt	James W. Taylor	0300883	Hq 3rd Inf Div
Capt	K. M. Bigelow	0344307	Hq XXI Corps
1st Lt	James E. Hawkins	01313602	46th QM GR Co

† Most of the enlisted-men witnesses represented various units of the 28th Division. (The execution was being staged for "maximum deterrent value" as well as to punish Private Slovik.) The complete list:

Sgt Milton W. Mueller	20221361	Co E, 110th Inf
Sgt Raymond F. Stivison	20305677	Co C, 110th Inf
Sgt George Patrick	12189289	Hq Co, 2nd Bn, 112th Inf
Sgt Victor F. Wahiani	33694101	Co M, 112th Inf
Sgt William J. Hagy	32071482	Btry B, 107th FA Bn

three doctors were at our right, about on a line with the position the firing squad was to take. While I didn't know him, no one could mistake Dr. Rougelot, with his height and mustache and with a stethoscope around his neck. Behind the wall that we faced rose this high, snow-covered hill, and I recall that I was impressed with the majesty of the whole setting. General Cota and his officers* moved in to the rear of us and to the right,

Sgt Millard B. Dunnam	34135259	Btry C, 107th FA Bn
Sgt Henry Guz	33050021	108th FA Bn
Sgt John S. Jankowski	37077353	108th FA Bn
Sgt Nick Cozik	20314261	109th FA Bn
Sgt Tony DiMichele	20313945	109th FA Bn
Sgt Henry F. Martin	20315934	Btry B, 229th FA Bn
Sgt Jackson B. Breish	20315935	Btry C, 229th FA Bn
Sgt James J. McGroerty	33022828	Co B, 103rd Engr (C) Bn
Sgt James W. Hess	20300531	28th MP Platoon
Sgt Frank J. McKendrick	33029048	28th MP Platoon
Sgt Robert E. Milbier	31097011	28th Hq Co
Sgt S. Keita	39025540	46th QM GR Co
Sgt Robert L. Broward	34024870	XXI Corps MP Platoon
Cpl Joseph L. Viteriae	32550293	Co A, 103rd Engr (C) Bn
Cpl Orrin W. Fluck	33028627	28th MP Platoon
Pfc Virgil M. Beetachen	36439173	28th MP Platoon
Pfc Auburn Nunkester	20303180	28th MP Platoon
Pfc Gerald A. Corwin	36743183	28th MP Platoon
Pfc Stephen J. French	36376600	28th MP Platoon
Pfc Joseph Byrnes	32600016	28th MP Platoon
Pfc Henry R. Jenkins	20306785	28th MP Platoon
Pfc Ray J. Stevens	16127274	28th MP Platoon
Pfc Harold E. Mitchell	20319621	28th MP Platoon
Pfc James L. Hardy	35497084	46th QM GR Co
Pfc Thomas W. Turner	35463848	46th QM GR Co
Pvt Russell Stanton	20300837	28th MP Platoon
Pvt James F. Shaughnessy	42130323	28th MP Platoon
Pvt Steve N. Buco	23060744	28th MP Platoon

* This group of officers, besides those already named as officiating, included:

Lt Col	James E. Rudder	0294916	Co 109th Inf
Lt Col	Herman A. Peters	0336122	Hq 28th Inf Div

near the house, and therefore General Cota was in a position to be first to see the "execution procession" as it moved out of the house and approached the post.

PRIVATE MORRISON: While we were standing there in the hall with our rifles Father Cummings came out and told us that he had been with Slovik and they had been through the usual Catholic proceedings with which I am not very well acquainted. He told us that he brought us a request from Slovik asking us to shoot straight and get it over with fast. I think this had a good effect on the firing squad. Nobody wanted to see Slovik suffer.

SERGEANT McKENDRICK: We used nylon rope — parachute-cord type — to tie up Slovik's hands before the procession started. We used the same sort of rope on his feet at the post. While I was tying his hands I said: "Take it easy, Eddie. Try to make it easy on yourself . . . and on us." He looked at me calmly and said: "I'm

Major	Vincent Keator	021283	Hq 28th Inf Div
Capt	John M. Cookenbach	0461636	Hq 28th Inf Div
Capt	Robert J. Hummel	0423785	Hq 103rd Engr (C) Bn
Capt	Herbert L. Franklin	01173952	Btry A, 107th FA Bn
Major	William F. Thomas	0396646	103rd Engr (C) Bn
Major	N. B. S. Thompson	0123089	Hq 28th Inf Div
Capt	Joseph L. Minter	040820242	109th FA Bn
1st Lt	Clark E. Miller	0447467	Hq 28th Inf Div
1st Lt	Paul M. Gallagher	0487002	Hq 28th Inf Div
1st Lt	Charles Stanceu	01295618	Co M, 110th Inf
1st Lt	Michael Duda	01321109	Co B, 112th Inf
1st Lt	James W. Hagood	01163699	108th FA Bn
1st Lt	James B. Carter	01175069	Btry B, 229th FA Bn
1st Lt	Brice E. Hall	01101855	Hq 103rd Engr (C) Bn

okay. They're not shooting me for deserting the United States Army. Thousands of guys have done that. They just need to make an example out of somebody and I'm it because I'm an ex-con. I use to steal things when I was a kid, and that's what they are shooting me for. They're shooting me for bread and chewing gum I stole when I was twelve years old."

—— While we were there in the hall Fellman came up and told Slovik that he was sorry but that he would have to read him that order again while he was standing at the post, and it was cold out there. "That's all right, Major," Slovik said. "I've heard it so many times, one more time won't do any harm. But read fast, will you?"

—— It was then that I put the OD blanket around his shoulders, to keep him from getting too cold while the order was being read. I took the blanket off when Hess and I were tying him to the post.

GENERAL COTA: "Attention!"

It was 9:56 A.M. The execution procession was moving out of the main hall, into the garden, and toward the post. Major Fellman and Father Cummings led, side by side. Then came Slovik, bareheaded, the blanket around his shoulders, his wrists bound, and two nylon ropes leading back to the hands of Hess and McKendrick, who walked behind him. Bringing up the rear was Private White, carrying the "collapse board."

[228   ]

CAPTAIN HUMMEL: I was standing right behind General Cota. I'll never forget how quiet it was. All you could hear were those feet sliding through the snow. Father Cummings's lips were moving in prayer, as were Slovik's. As they reached the post, Slovik turned around, and the chaplain, Hess and McKendrick stood there with him while Fellman stepped back. Then Fellman, in his command voice that could be heard all over the courtyard, told Slovik that it was his duty as officer in charge of the execution to read him the order. Fellman read rapidly. . . . I guess it took him two or three minutes — Elbeuf, Rocherath, Cota, Eisenhower . . . Slovik must have heard it fifty times.

DOCTOR ROUGELOT: That boy had the bluest eyes I ever saw. I'll never forget how blue they looked as he stood there at the post while Fellman was reading the order . . . with that snow-banked hill behind him. His lips were moving in prayer.

FATHER CUMMINGS: Slovik was repeating prayers known to every Catholic. The Act of Contrition:

. . . . O my God, I am heartily sorry for having offended thee, and I detest all my sins. . . .

. . . . Mother of Mercy, pray for us.

. . . . Most Sacred Heart of Jesus, have mercy on us.

[229   ]

. . . . Jesus, Mary and Joseph, bless us now at the hour of our death.

MAJOR FELLMAN: "Private Slovik, do you have a statement to make before the order directing your execution is carried out?"

SLOVIK: "No."

FATHER CUMMINGS: (*addressing the prisoner in a strong voice*) "Private Slovik, do you have a last statement to make to me, as a chaplain, before your death?"

SLOVIK: "No, Father."

FELLMAN: "Prepare the condemned for execution."

SERGEANT McKENDRICK: We bound his ankles with the nylon rope, and to strap him to the post we used those web belts that come on officers' bedrolls. We put the straps around and under each shoulder and around the post, and we caught them on that spike in the back of the post to keep him from slumping. Then we strapped him around the knees and around the ankles. He couldn't have fallen. While we were strapping him, the chaplain was repeating prayers with him. When we had him strapped good, I took out the hood and stepped up to put it on him.

[230   ]

FATHER CUMMINGS: Just before McKendrick pulled the hood over his head, I said to him: "Eddie, when you get Up There, say a little prayer for me." He answered: "Okay, Father. I'll pray that you don't follow me too soon." Those were his last words to any of us as the hood came down.

It was 10:01 A.M. Lieutenant Koziak's voice could be heard from the hall ordering the firing squad to march. He brought them out in quick step, rifles At Trail, in a single file, halted them in the path dug for them, and faced them toward Slovik. They brought their rifles to Port and Unlocked.

SERGEANT McKENDRICK: Hess and I took cover in a small house, a sort of gardener's workhouse, about twenty feet to the left of the post.

COLONEL ELSON: The firing squad was standing so close in front of me that I could almost reach out and touch one of the boys on the shoulder.

PRIVATE MORRISON: When we marched in Slovik was there strapped to the post with the hood on. I watched him closely for any sign of emotion, but brother there was none. He was standing there as straight as could be. If there had been any movement on his part I sure would have seen it. I had steeled myself for the job and my nerve was steady. I was cold and wanted to get it over with and get in out of the weather. I didn't imagine that Slovik was enjoying the waiting either.

MAJOR FELLMAN: "Squad . . . Ready . . . Aim . . . FIRE!"

CAPTAIN HUMMEL: I don't believe anybody who was there will ever forget one thing: the sharp crack of that volley echoing across the snow in those hills, followed by an almost perfect silence. Not a sound.

PRIVATE MORRISON: When I fired that cook's rifle, the barrel must have been partly stopped up and the rest of the way dirty. It spun me almost halfway around on the firing line and almost broke my collarbone. I can safely say I didn't have a blank.

CAPTAIN HUMMEL: The first action that broke that terrible silence was Rougelot walking slowly up to put his stethoscope to Slovik's heart. With his six feet three inches of height, the snow broke under every step he took, and that's all you could hear: just that crushing snow. It seemed to me he walked a mile.

SERGEANT MCKENDRICK: Slovik had slumped forward, and he may have been unconscious, but he wasn't dead. Every man in the courtyard saw him struggle up at least twice.

DOCTOR ROUGELOT: The shooting had been very poor and reflected the nervousness of the riflemen. Not one of the bullets had struck the heart. The wounds ranged from high in the neck region out to the left shoulder, over the left chest, and under the heart. One bullet was in the left upper arm. But there had been no intentional misses; all eleven bullets were in the body. Perhaps I had been wrong in not following the suggestion that a paper target be pinned over the heart. Since these riflemen were used to killing human beings, I had discounted the emotional effect resulting from the requirement of killing one of their own buddies. Perhaps the paper target would have given a better result.

COLONEL ELSON: I had the impression that the shooting might have been better if the firing squad had been handled a little more deliberately. It seemed to me that the boys wheeled in, faced about, and fired, all within the space of a few seconds.

DOCTOR ROUGELOT: I applied the stethoscope to the man's chest. His body was quivering slightly; his breathing was extremely shallow; the heartbeat faint, rapid, and irregular. It was obvious that the man would be dead in a few moments, and I felt that by the time I withdrew and the soldiers fired again the second volley would be unnecessary. I therefore continued auscultation of the heart, expecting its momentary cessation. These moments were harrowing for everybody, and a few short words were spoken. Fellman gave the order to

[233]

reload, and the chaplain spoke curtly to him: "Give him another volley if you like it so much!" And I restrained the chaplain with something like: "Take it easy, Padre, none of us is enjoying this."

Lieutenant Koziak passed rapidly behind the firing squad, reloading the rifles. Each rifleman, keeping his face forward so as not to see the shell enter the chamber, pushed his rifle backward for the reloading.

COLONEL ELSON: While the young lieutenant was reloading the rifles, I noticed that he, in his haste, was pointing them directly toward the enlisted-men witnesses. This caused me to speak my only informal words. In a voice that only a few could hear, I said: "Be careful, Lieutenant. Let's not kill one of our own *accidentally* here this morning."

Neither Major Fellman nor Lieutenant Koziak heard the remarks of Chaplain Cummings and Colonel Elson.

MAJOR FELLMAN: Koziak had almost finished loading, so I ordered Major Rougelot to either pronounce the man dead or else stand back for the second volley . . . in accordance with the SOP.

DOCTOR ROUGELOT: "The second volley won't be necessary, Major. Private Slovik is dead."

GENERAL COTA: That was the roughest fifteen minutes of my life.

[234   ]

SERGEANT McKENDRICK: While the courtyard emptied rapidly, Hess and I cut the body down, and Father Cummings began anointing it with the oil. I believe the other Catholic chaplain, Lieutenant Colonel Ralph E. Smith, helped him. I pulled off the right shoe and sock so the chaplain could anoint the feet. Then the Graves Registration detail took over, went through his pockets, pulled off one of his dogtags, and slipped him into a mattress cover.

CAPTAIN HUMMEL: I walked over to McKendrick and pointed to that "collapse board" that we had built: it was standing there against that little flower house. "It turned out that we didn't need that bit of apparatus, did we?" I said. "No, not Slovik," Mac replied. "I came nearer needing it than he did. I can't figure that guy out. If he was a coward he certainly didn't show it today."

FATHER CUMMINGS: Slovik was the bravest man in the garden that morning.

PRIVATE MORRISON: Slovik had nerve. I can't understand why a man who had the guts to face a firing squad like that wouldn't stay in the line with the rest of us. I honestly believe that he thought they would not execute him but would give him a dishonorable discharge.

FATHER CUMMINGS: If you ask me where Eddie Slovik

[235]

found his courage, I'll have to give you the "commercial." For two thousand years the Catholic Church has been supplying what Eddie Slovik needs on the day he meets his death. From where else can a little man find strength?

By 10:30 A.M., just three hours after his arrival in St. Marie, a high-priority SECRET TWX had been transmitted to Paris:

TO: COMMANDING GENERAL, ETOUSA
FROM: HQ, 28TH INF DIV
   PURSUANT TO GCMO 27 HEADQUARTERS ETOUSA 23 JAN 45, PRIVATE EDDIE D. SLOVIK, 36896415, FORMERLY COMPANY G, 109TH INF, WAS SHOT TO DEATH BY A FIRING SQUAD AT 1005 HOURS, 31 JAN 45 AT ST. MARIE AUX MINES, FRANCE.
                         COTA

The case of *The United States vs. Private Slovik* was closed.

In Retrospect . . .

HERE, briefly, an attempt will be made to answer some of the questions which may remain in the minds of thoughtful readers who consider this case.

Why was not the President of the United States involved? Why did not President Roosevelt exercise the final authority?

This is the point on which Antoinette Slovik is unreconciled. She says: "I remember reading in high school about how wives and mothers had the opportunity to appeal to President Lincoln in such cases. I not only was denied this opportunity, I was not even informed that my husband was under sentence of death."

Throughout virtually all our national history the power of life and death over American soldiers has been exclusively the President's — the constitutional commander in chief. But by an Act of Congress (Act of June 4, 1920, 41 stat 787, as amended) confirming power was

[237   ]

delegated to the theater commanders in certain death cases, one of which was desertion in time of war.

Therefore, President Roosevelt was not involved; and there is nothing in the records to indicate that he was ever informed of the decision to execute a deserter.

If this power had remained in the hands of the President, would Slovik have been executed?

No. No informed person with whom I talked would answer otherwise. The President of the United States is elected by civilians, and the distance between civil life and a battle line is too great. Slovik was shot in 1945 only because the final decision was in the hands of a soldier.

Two cases in point: the Lichfield case and the case of another deserter sentenced to death by a 28th Division general court.

The scum of the American army was confined in the stockade of the 10th Replacement Depot at Lichfield, England: murderers, rapists, the most flagrant deserters. This depot was commanded by a fine officer, Colonel James Kilian. Shortly after the war some of these criminals, seeking freedom, charged that they had been "beaten up" and "mistreated" by sergeants in the stockade.

The most vociferous public opinion was entirely in favor of the criminals: the blood of Kilian was demanded. In the longest court-martial in American history Colonel Kilian was exonerated of all the serious charges; but when the army submitted his name to Congress for promotion President Truman could not withstand the pressure. He denied Colonel Kilian promotion, passed him over. This was a great victory for the deserters and those who supported them.

In the 28th Division's most flagrant desertion case, a sergeant left the line in Germany, bought forged papers in Paris to get to London, where he bought papers which enabled him to reach his home in Chicago. He turned himself in to MPs in the last days of the war, confident — as Slovik had been — that he would soon be free.

In September, 1945, at Camp Shelby, Mississippi, he was tried — with six wounded combat veterans sitting on the court. They gave him death. The response was a call from Washington: "The President wants no more death sentences for desertion. You must therefore reconvene the court and change the sentence to life imprisonment."

The members of the court objected, insisted that they be allowed to record the death sentence, then let the President take the responsibility for clemency. But the President didn't want this responsibility; and the court reluctantly complied with the instructions.*

* In reviewing this, the Army Office of Public Information commented: "There is no record in the Judge Advocate General's office of any phone calls made from Washington to Camp Shelby in connection with any case to which Mr. Huie may be referring here."

That deserter is now a free man . . . just as Slovik expected to be.

Was the United States under any obligation, legal or otherwise, to notify Antoinette Slovik that her husband was under sentence of death?

The army legal authorities say no: Slovik was at liberty to inform his wife by letter, and the choice was his. The army regards every able-bodied citizen-soldier as his own master; it volunteers no information about his difficulties even to his next of kin. If the next of kin inquires about a suspected difficulty, the army will reply with the facts. But the initiative is never taken by the army.

Army authorities hold that to follow any other policy would be to break faith with the individual soldier.

Was Slovik's case the most flagrant case of avoidance of duty during the Second War?

Few persons who are familiar with other cases contend that it was. There were cases involving officers — men with fine backgrounds, and therefore, it would seem, with a greater degree of responsibility to the United States than Eddie Slovik. Some of these were sentenced to death, their sentences were approved by the convening authority, but they were never shot. Instead, most of them are now free, and at least one has had his full citizenship rights restored.

But if Slovik was shot, and if forty-eight others received approved death sentences, why was not at least one other deserter shot?

As Colonel Stevens has pointed out in this text, there was a "hue and cry" even in the army after the Slovik execution. A coward or a deserter can't be quietly hanged or electrocuted in the privacy of a jail: if his death is to be a deterrent he must be killed by and in the view of the men he failed. And, as anyone who has read the description of the Slovik execution can see, this is "harrowing business."

General Eisenhower *confirmed* one other death sentence for desertion, after Slovik's, but he never got around to ordering it carried out.

Perhaps the best explanation as to why Slovik's execution was the first and last is this: There were many Americans who believed that flagrant deserters must be shot, but nobody wanted the job.

Was General Eisenhower the only American theater commander who had to deal with the desertion problem?

No, but he was the principal one, for several reasons. General Eisenhower commanded our "mass" effort in the Second War. All other commanders were responsible for relatively small numbers of men.

Desertion was not a major problem in the Pacific for obvious reasons. It was essentially an air and naval war;

small bodies of infantry were employed; there were no long periods of static warfare; the conditions for desertion did not exist.

It was during the long, bitter winters of static warfare in Italy, France, and Germany that the desertion problem became acute. Therefore, it was largely a problem for General Eisenhower's command.

Should Antoinette Slovik have received the $10,000 service insurance carried by her husband? And should she receive it now?

Under the Insurance Act of 1940 the money cannot be paid. The law says:

No insurance shall be payable for death inflicted as lawful punishment for crime.

But Antoinette Slovik's position is this: She insists that her husband did not suffer death "inflicted as lawful punishment for crime." The fact that no other offender was "punished" in the same manner indicates to her that her husband was put to death as an "example" . . . as a "disciplinary measure." She points to the Bertolet-Betts review:

If the death penalty is ever to be imposed for desertion it should be imposed in this case, not as a punitive measure nor as a retribution, but to maintain that discipline upon which alone an army can succeed against the enemy.

To her, that means that Eddie Slovik was not shot to death as a "punitive measure"; therefore, the above law does not apply in her case, and the Veterans Administration has no right to withhold payment of the insurance.

She further points to General Cota's action in approving "only so much of the sentence as provides that the accused be shot to death with musketry" as indicating that the general, carefully and intentionally, acted to make it possible for her to receive, not only the insurance, but also the "accumulated pay and allowances."

She will ask the Congress of the United States to direct the court of claims to pay her the insurance plus the accumulated pay and allowances. Whether she gets it or not will depend, chiefly, on the attitude of the veterans' organizations — and on the President.

In the years since the execution have there been any changes in attitude among the principals in the case?

DOCTOR KIMMELMAN: "A few weeks after I had voted for the death sentence for Slovik as a member of the court, I was captured in the Bulge battle, and didn't know of his execution until after my release from a German prison camp. In prison, we often talked about the case. I can't say positively what I would have done if I had still been with the division in January, 1945, but the experiences in the Battle of the Bulge altered my views. I came to believe front-line offenses ought to be judged only by front-line personnel. At trial time, we had not been a court of front-line personnel. He got a fair trial under the circumstances, but in retrospect, the circumstances were not fair. I believe I would have tried to do whatever was in my power to get the entire case reviewed on this basis."

MAJOR BERTOLET: "I still believe that the cause of the United States was well served in the Slovik execution."

LIEUTENANT COLONEL STEVENS: "I am still firmly convinced that military justice of a very high order was accomplished in his execution."

PRIVATE TANKEY: "Eddie Slovik was a goodhearted guy. He never hurt anybody in his life. He helped me; he helped everybody. He was a poor kid who had had a raw deal. It's wrong to kill a man like that."

PRIVATE MORRISON: "I'm sorry for Slovik, but I still say he got what he deserved. I'm just sorry that others like him didn't get the same treatment. If everybody had acted like he did, we'd be living under Hitler today. And I think General Eisenhower's plan worked. It helped to stiffen a few backbones. When the report of the execution was read to my company formation, the effect was good. It made a lot of guys think about what it means to be an American. I'm just sorry the general didn't follow through and shoot the rest of the deserters instead of turning them loose on their communities. I want my children to be raised to believe that this country is worth dying for . . . and that if they won't fight for it, they don't deserve to live."

COLONEL RUDDER: "I still feel as I did the day I published the order in behalf of the execution of Private Slovik."

GENERAL COTA: "During the Second World War I was charged by the people of the United States with the responsibility of leading American troops whose mission it was to destroy the German army. I was privileged to lead thirty-six thousand Americans into battle, and I saw many of them die for the principles in which we believe. Given the same conditions of those hours, I do not see how I could have acted differently in the Slovik case and remained faithful to my responsibilities. I have only one regret: I regret that Private Slovik had to be a product of our replacement system. This was a cruel system, probably necessitated by the nature of the war, but it was cruel, nevertheless, and I never liked it. Men have a right to go into battle as members of a trained unit, flanked by friends and associates, and, if possible, led by leaders who have trained them and whom they have come to trust. To thrust an individual, no matter how well trained as an individual he may be, into battle as a member of a strange unit is in my opinion expecting

[245]

more than many men are capable of giving. I'm glad that the army is now moving in this direction."

In the event war is resumed is it possible for another American deserter or coward to be shot as was Slovik?

It is still possible . . . theoretically. But all the changes in military law since 1945 have tended toward making it a practical improbability. There is now provision for appeal to a United States Court of Military Appeals, composed of three civilian judges. Such a case, under the new laws, could be delayed for months; therefore, it is most improbable that a death sentence would ever be ordered into execution.

So, while army authorities shudder to have it said, it would be difficult to challenge a prediction that Private Eddie Slovik will have been the *only* American put to death for avoidance of duty between 1864 and the year, somewhere in the future, when the United States ceases to be free.

Thus the final, inescapable question which the Slovik case poses for every thoughtful American:

What of DUTY today? And what of AVOIDANCE of duty? In a world in which each generation must still, by force of arms, maintain its right to be free, how can we make certain that enough young Americans will honor their duty to the United States and be willing to make the efforts and the sacrifices?

If the Slovik case can contribute to understanding and resolution on this point, then a depression kid who never had much chance — and who must sleep the eternal sleep in the dishonored plot at Fère-en-Tardenois — will, in death, have served the cause of America.

Postscript . . .

In writing this book, the author had the full cooperation of the Department of the Army, which checked every page for accuracy. According to the military law in effect during World War II, the Commander of a War Theater had to take final action in cases involving death sentences for military crimes. The court-martial imposed the sentence, the convening authority approved the sentence, and the Theater Commander made his decision on their recommendations and issued the necessary instructions for carrying it out. Soon after World War II, this regulation in the military code was changed, and the President of the United States is now responsible for the final review of death sentences, making it likely that Eddie Slovik's death will remain the last military execution of an American soldier for desertion of duty.

After the war, the Army never informed Antoinette Slovik of the nature of her husband's death, and the letter written to her by Chaplain Cummings explaining the last moments of her husband's life and offering his condolences was kept in a secret file in the Pentagon. Believing he died honorably, Antoinette notified the Michigan Reformatory, which placed a gold star beside his name. In 1954, when the world first learned about Slovik's execution, that star was removed. Antoinette Slovik continued to wear the simple wedding band that her husband gave her before going overseas, and she spent the rest of her life trying to clear his name. According to General Cota, he approved the death sentence only after Army lawyers assured him that if Slovik was executed his widow would receive the National Service Life insurance benefits. He was stunned to learn that they were never paid.

Despite the efforts of William Bradford Huie, who spent decades trying to get the benefits for Slovik's widow, in 1977 the Army offered sympathy but rejected her claim for $10,000 and interest in life insurance benefits. They also rejected her request to have her husband's remains returned to the United States from an unmarked grave in France. Congress upheld both of those decisions. In 1978, President Jimmy Carter was unsuccessful in intervening on her behalf. Antoinette Slovik, crippled and indigent, died a year later in a Detroit hospital, one week before the Senate was scheduled to vote on changing Slovik's service record so that she could receive his insurance benefits. Bernard V. Calka, a World War II veteran, continued to pursue Slovik's case and, in 1987, the Army finally acquiesced and allowed Eddie Slovik's remains to be returned to the United States to be buried beside Antoinette's.